Dancing Spirits

Also by Iris Laine

Getting to Know God

If you've outgrown your childhood God...
Get to know the God you'll never outgrow (2001)

Promotion in Foodservice

(Co-Author: College Text with Workbook, 1972)

Dancing Spirits

✦

Quantum Physics and Religion…Fact and Faith Offer Hope and Joy Here and Hereafter

Iris Laine, M.Div.

iUniverse, Inc.
New York Lincoln Shanghai

Dancing Spirits
Quantum Physics and Religion...Fact and Faith Offer Hope and Joy Here and Hereafter

iUniverse books may be ordered through booksellers or by contacting:

iUniverse
2021 Pine Lake Road, Suite 100
Lincoln, NE 68512
www.iuniverse.com
1-800-Authors (1-800-288-4677)

Background Cover Photograph: "Points of Light" by Fred Casselman

ISBN-13: 978-0-595-40516-9 (pbk)
ISBN-13: 978-0-595-84882-9 (ebk)
ISBN-10: 0-595-40516-9 (pbk)
ISBN-10: 0-595-84882-6 (ebk)

Printed in the United States of America

Dedication

To my husband, Steve, with whose Spirit my Spirit longs to dance eternally as gracefully and grace-giving as they have danced together for many happy years.

To all my "Dancing Spirit" sisters and brothers with whom Steve and I visited when I served as Volunteer Visitation Minister for our church, only to find they were more of a blessing to us than we ever could be to them.

To Suzanne, who has been a true inspiration, whose Spirit I look forward to seeing dance in hope and joy here and hereafter.

To all my loved ones, children, family and friends, who have loved me even when I was unlovable…tolerated me when I was intolerable…and whose Spirits danced with mine in selfless grace even when my Spirit insisted on trying to lead.

Contents

From the Author...

If I could put together all the bits and pieces of everything I have learned from my spiritual faith, from scientific facts and from ordinary folks in times of fear and anxiety, it would be like a Manual for Dancing Spirits. That's what this book is all about.

It is my effort to apply some of the latest in scientific facts to the spiritual faith I must have been blessed with even before my earliest childhood memories. Its sole purpose is to ease fears and anxieties about life here and hereafter, to reveal the everlasting Spirit within each of us and to energize that Spirit so it literally dances in hope and joy.

Read it with an open mind and an open heart. It can awaken your everlasting Spirit and give it that same energy and joy in life that an exhilarating dance can give. And in that experience, it is my hope and prayer you will recognize your spiritual faith is actually based on proven fact.

1

Come Dance with Me!

"Praise the Lord!
Sing to the Lord a new song, his praise in the
    assembly of the faithful!
Let them praise his name with dancing,
    making melody to him with timbrel and lyre!"

—Psalms 149:1, 3

The practice of dancing in praise of God dates back many centuries. One of the most memorable examples in ancient times was the story of King David when he successfully brought the Ark of the Covenant to its rightful place in the City of David.

"So David went and brought up the ark of God…to the city of David with
rejoicing; and when those who bore the ark of the Lord had gone six paces,
he sacrificed an ox and a fatling. And David danced before the Lord with
all his might…"

—2 Samuel 6:12b-14

While out of favor for many years as a way to relate to God, dancing has again become a Christian expression of one's faith and a way to praise God. It is prayerfully done in many churches, especially on important Christian occasions. Best of all, it can help to reinforce our faith. Science and religion join together to suggest that life itself can be a dance in praise of God.

The research of the past century in Quantum Physics, or Quantum Mechanics as it is also known, illustrates that our invisible Spirit or Soul, which we all believe we have, may actually dance eternally. What is even more interesting is that living in selfless love of others, as Jesus both taught and lived out on earth, can encourage our own invisible Spirit to dance more gracefully and, as it does, spread an aura of light and energy on those around us. The result is that we experience more joy in this life and we're blessed with more hope for joy in our life hereafter.

If you're wondering by now what kind of an expert I am to make such claims, please accept my confession up front. I'm no physicist. Science was never my best subject. I'm a lifelong Lutheran, born, baptized, confirmed and married in the strictest of Lutheran circles. For eight years I attended Lutheran elementary school and committed to memory hundreds of Bible passages. They are etched on my brain in the words of the original King James translation of the Bible for infinity, I'm sure.

The first major crisis point in my lifelong commitment to Lutheranism came in a class in Ancient Roman History in my sophomore year in college. Imagine my amazement when the professor told of religions which existed before Christianity. There were virgin births, angels who sang at them, a savior who died, returned and would do so again. After class I questioned him, thinking I had misunderstood. No, all he covered was well authenticated.

For the next six months I spent every spare moment in the university library reading up on world religions. Through the previous years from early high school on, I had struggled through what I had learned in eight years of Lutheran elementary school. Some of it just didn't seen fair and right in our multi-cultural world. Yet, what one learns so well from ages five through thirteen is not so easily put aside.

That exposure to ancient world religions left its indelible mark on me, but for the next thirty-five years I was caught up in the needs of daily living. I married and was blest with a daughter, then divorced and struggled as a single mother. Eventually I married again and have been blessed with both a wonderful husband and stepchildren. In my early fifties, our children grown, my husband and I moved from the midwest to Florida and started our own small business. We also joined the largest Lutheran church in town. While my husband was happy and active there, I became increasingly frustrated. More than ever, I felt the need to move from a strictly Lutheran view of God and the Spirit to a broader, more all-encompassing view of life.

With my husband's blessing, I enrolled in Harvard Divinity School, followed by a year at St. Vincent de Paul Catholic Seminary near home, a chaplaincy at a local, mainly Jewish, hospital and ultimately graduated from the Lutheran Seminary in Gettysburg, Pennsylvania. I was in my early sixties when ordained. Over the years I served several Lutheran churches in south Florida, preached at even more of them as well as at a Catholic Seminary Chapel and a Unitarian Fellowship. My goal was to share the love of God from a Christian perspective. Following retirement from active ministry I first wrote my faith autobiography, *Getting to Know God*, published in 2001. Then I volunteered as Visitation Minister for the Lutheran Church of which we were members. With the help of husband Steve, we visited hospitals, nursing and rehabilitation facilities as well as those folks who were ill or disabled and confined to their homes. We brought hugs and kisses, counsel, prayer and Holy Communion, whatever was needed.

The more we prayed with our "shut-in" friends, the more I was plagued by just how prayer worked in a practical sense. How did it help someone to be free of fear and anxiety about the future? Those thoughts drove me back to ideas I had years before. Does prayer create thought waves, like sound and light waves? We send out prayers to ask for help. As Christians we pray to God the Father, to Jesus the Son and to the Holy Spirit. Followers of other religions pray to God as they understand and relate to the supreme source of life.

I began searching the internet for information on prayer as thought waves and found I wasn't original. Some professionals were already researching the power and success of thought waves, called "thotons." The name was given to subatomic entities believed to make up thought waves, just as "photons" make up light waves. That lead to more research, and I began reading articles and books on Quantum Mechanics. Two of them in particular showed a relationship between the research of the last century and ancient Eastern religions. My own religious studies, especially of Judaism and Christianity, suggested a relationship to Western religions as well.

I tried sharing with some of the "shut-ins" on whom we called the ideas that kept nudging their way into my consciousness as a result of all this study. There was a widow who had lost her husband of more than sixty years, a friend my daughter's age who because of a debilitating stroke couldn't eat or speak normally, a widow who suffered from constant and intense pain, a beautiful elderly friend who could barely see. What I had to share with them of my newly found insights into our spiritual life seemed to bring them additional comfort. It reinforced their faith in the promises of God, given us through the words of Jesus.

One of the intriguing ideas in Quantum Mechanics research emphasized a basic tenet of Eastern religions. It revealed the entire universe moved in a kind of dance. The tiny entities in the atoms which make up all matter are in constant motion, creating new forms and giving off energy. Just so, each individual person is constantly changing, hopefully growing in wisdom while giving off love, actually energizing and improving their own life and that of those around them.

In a very few moments in my life I have had the excitement of dancing with utter abandon. Maybe you too have found excitement in dancing, or in some other activity that you can no longer do, which brought you pleasure and fulfill-ment. Now, no way would I like to keep up a constant whirling movement but the emotion dancing aroused in me was like a new energy and excitement for life. If we are Spirit at the core of our earthly body, what I like to call our bio-body suit, our Spirit should be able to dance and experience that same new energy and excitement for life even if we're plagued with pain, anxieties and fear of the future.

Keep in mind, by dancing I don't mean the sometimes awkward and stilted way some of us move on the dance floor nor a constant exhausting purposeless whirling. Rather, I mean a grace-filled movement of growth toward what we sometimes speak of as Godliness. That's the true and ultimate dance of life, when we reach out in love, even sacrificial love, toward another. As Christians, we think immediately and especially of Jesus. For others it may be the Buddha, Moham-med, Krishna or even individuals like Mahatma Gandhi, Sister Teresa, St. Fran-cis, the disciples of Jesus and so many others. The dance of each was indeed the dance of life we can all use as our guide. We, too, can dance through life so that our inner Spirit, that core of our bio-body suit we often call our Soul, transcends reality. We can sense that joy which comes when we give off the energy of love and actually change the world around us.

If I could do that for you, this book will really be a Manual for Dancing Spir-its. And the sheer magic of it will be that it won't matter how well you dance now or whether your body is agile and graceful. The Manual for Dancing Spirits will help you to dance spiritually now and know that when your eternal Spirit or Soul is free of your body you will dance then with unbelievable skill and grace. Best of all, it will be a never-ending dance, an eternity of giving and receiving love, of growing in wisdom and Godliness. That thought can give us all, no matter how difficult our circumstances are now, a true reason to feel happy and hopeful here now and as we look ahead.

So I invite you to come and dance with me. With God's help, I will do my best to put together this Manual for Dancing Spirits. Of course, we all perceive of God, that Divine Master of the Universe, in different ways, depending on where we were born and what our religion is. Christians like me believe in God as a trin-ity of Father, Son and Spirit. American Indians think of God as the Great Spirit. Writers of the movie script for 2001 referred to God as The Force. What you will discover as you read is that religion and science have much in common. They began in the murky mists of many millennia past, in scattered centers of peoples across our earth all asking the same questions, all creating their own stories to explain the mysteries of life and death, all searching for meaning. Now, in the twenty-first century, religion and science are coming together. The latest in scientific research and proven spiritual insight can come together for you, can bring you new hope to set your Spirit dancing.

The first task is to explain and review the latest scientific research and, honestly, that seemed like an insurmountable accomplishment for me. First I had to understand it. Then I had to be able to explain it to you and, unfortunately, science has never been my strong suit. Hopefully, I understand some basics now well enough to share them with you. And if I can understand them, so can you. Believe me, it's worth it. For the first time ever, I believe fact and faith come together. That conviction has brought me a special kind of joy and a peace and contentment that I wish to share. Just keep in mind, our goal is for your eternal, everlasting, ever-loving Spirit and mine to dance hopefully and joyfully now and forever.

Here we go! You are about to enter the world of Quantum Physics, also known as Quantum Theory or Quantum Mechanics. We'll review the research of the past century, not as a physicist would, not as a learned theologian, but from the viewpoint of the average believer in God and in the promises of our faith. Just remember, each of us is more than our earthly body, the bio-body suit God has given us for our life on earth. And, if you're like me, your bio-body suit isn't what it once was. No matter though, it's only a "cover-all" for the happy, lively dancing Spirit that is the real you! So put aside your doubts, your aches and anxieties. Come and dance with me!

2

Quantum Physics Tells Us Why We Dance

The general notions about human understanding...which
are illustrated by discoveries in atomic physics are not
in the nature of things wholly unfamiliar... What we find
is an exemplification, an encouragement, and a refinement
of old wisdom.

—Julius Robert Oppenheimer
Science and the Common Understanding

Some of the great physicists of our time have recognized that research findings in Quantum Physics, the study of subatomic entities, are simply another expression of what has been known for many centuries, even as expressed in both ancient and contemporary religion. The quote which opens this chapter gives evidence of that.

There are two individuals in particular who recognized this and wrote books about it, making a very complex subject readable and understandable, even to a science novice like me. Without them I would not have been able to pursue the subject further by reading additional books and articles and I certainly could not have written this book.

As suggested previously, I was convinced of the idea that prayer consisted of thought waves which were similar to light and sound waves but which we still do not yet understand.

To study physics at my age seemed impossible, so I pushed the idea to the back of my mind. Then, as a result of a discussion with my daughter, I discovered *The Dancing Wu Li Masters* by Gary Zukav, and shortly thereafter *The Tao of Physics* written by Fritjof Capra. Both give a popular view of Quantum Physics, also known as Quantum Theory or Quantum Mechanics, and its relation to ancient Eastern religions. I read and reread them. The result was that I came to the conclusion not only did there appear to be a relationship between Quantum Mechanics and Eastern religions but with Western religions, especially including Christianity, as well.

Since both books were published some twenty-five years ago, however, I began additional research in books and articles written more recently. Amongst the best was *The Quantum World* by Kenneth W. Ford, published in 2004. His chapter titled "How Small is Small? How Fast is Fast?" is an ideal introduction to the fundamental entities studied in Quantum Physics which impact us physically and, in my estimation, spiritually as well.

What became fascinating for me as I read is that physicists are no different than theologians. They differ widely in their beliefs, the theories constructed based on those beliefs, and the tests conducted to prove those theories. Before we delve into them, however, there are just a couple of basics to keep in mind as we review the relationship between facts and faith, science and spirituality.

To begin with, Quantum Physics and faith or spirituality do not speak the same language. The Bible, originally composed in Hebrew and Greek, is available in a number of different translations in English. While physicists may gain inspiration and ideas from intuition and imagination, Quantum Physics actually communicates in mathematical formulas.

A basic but profound example is Albert Einstein's formula: $E=MC^2$. E stands for energy, M stands for mass or matter and C is the speed of light which is 186,000 miles per second. So, in everyday easy-to-understand language, if you weigh 200 pounds, the energy that you represent is equal to 200 times 186,000 squared or times itself. Specifically, the energy you represent is 200 times 186,000 times 186,000. That's a lot of energy and a startling fact simply expressed in a mathematical formula.

Faith or spirituality definitely isn't expressed in mathematics. It speaks in myths, symbols and introspective experiences. Our Bible is full of myths. A myth, incidentally, isn't a made-up story, a fairy tale. Rather it's a symbolic story of how we understand ourselves, our origin, our reason for being, our relationship to each other and our destiny. It's not important that the story is not historically true. It's important only in that it truly signifies our deepest beliefs.

When it comes to symbols, the most well-known Christian symbol is the cross. It is not only a symbol of sacrificial love, Jesus of Nazareth dying for all, but an historical event.

Lastly, our faith is nurtured through introspection, or what we call prayer or meditation. In prayer, we talk to God. We ask for help for ourselves, for our loved ones, for the world. We compliment or praise God. We acknowledge our mistakes, give thanks for God's grace, God's love which we don't deserve, and we ask for help to do better.

When we talk to God, we're talking to a spirit, an invisible entity. Invisible entity is not an oxymoron. An atom is invisible, for example, but it's very real. Even subatomic entities too small to be seen with a microscope are real. Invisibility does not mean non-existent. It may just be what we have not fully discovered yet but accept by faith or by telltale signs. We believe by faith that we have a Spirit or Soul. We can't see it but we can get in touch with it, just as in Quantum Physics researchers can't actually see subatomic entities but they see evidence of them.

Which brings us to meditation. Prayer is when we talk to God. Meditation, or centering prayer, is when we turn inward to listen for God's voice. It's when God, our Spirit Father, talks and we listen, something at which we're not always good. Listening is harder than talking,

Do our children listen to us, especially when they're teenagers? We should be so lucky. Now, don't we consider ourselves as God's children yet how often do we listen to God? We are admonished and encouraged in our churches, synagogues, temples and mosques to pray. I have to think that God, who is our Spirit Parent, must think sometimes, "Stop talking! Listen to Me!" That's what we do in meditation or centering prayer.

But let's get back to Quantum Physics. Those first two books I read and studied gave an extensive review of Quantum Physics and its relation to ancient religions. As indicated earlier, I soon learned that they were just a beginning. I began to explore the library, the bookstores and the internet. The major sources for my research are listed in the Reference Section of this book. Since I'm not a physicist and assume that most of my readers are not either, the explanations and conclusions reached are in my everyday language and reflect my understanding of the subject.

First, what exactly is Quantum Physics or Quantum Mechanics as it is often called. This is the question most people ask when the subject is mentioned. To begin with, physics is the study of mass or matter and of energy. Matter and energy are made up of atoms which are, in turn, made up of subatomic entities, so tiny they cannot be seen even with a microscope. Tiny as they are, these subatomic entities make up all of our world and they are in constant motion. This gives us the name Quantum Physics or Mechanics which refers to that motion. They are discrete quantities of subatomic entities in constant motion. I view them as the invisible essence of all matter and energy engaged in an everlasting dance. They are "Dancing Spirits."

So, for the purposes of understanding our "Dancing Spirits" from a factual or scientific viewpoint as well as from our faith or religious perspective, let's review the research in Quantum Physics during the last century. We will explore the world of dancing subatomic entities to see if they actually do point the way through science to what the religions of our world, and especially Christianity, have been trying to tell us all along.

Up until the beginning of the 20th century, when we talked about physics we meant Newtonian or what we may now call Classical Physics. It had been the foundation for understanding science since the 1600s when Isaac Newton made his significant discoveries. It was Newton who gave us a mechanical model for the universe through the laws of motion and gravity.

As a result of Newton's findings we could actually predict events in our physical world. For example, we could predict where a moving object was going, actually determining just where and at what time a specific material entity or mass would be located. Without Newton's work, the space program would not have been possible. This gave humans a feeling of being a separate and independent entity apart from the matter they studied. Actually, Quantum Mechanics may indicate that we are a part of the universal whole, not apart from it, as you will soon discover.

In order to illustrate his findings in precise mathematics so physicists could communicate more easily, Newton had to invent a new mathematical method. It is called differential calculus. No, you don't have to understand calculus. We'll work our way around it.

Newton's physics assumed that our world consisted of small, solid and indestructible particles of which all matter or mass was made. Further, he believed that their position in time and in space was determined by the laws of motion and gravity.

By the beginning of the 20th century a complete theory of electromagnetism had also been developed. This explained phenomena that were not covered by Newton's mechanical theories. Then, in the 20th century two new developments totally changed how physicists viewed the world in which we live. One was the work of Albert Einstein in what are known as the special and the general theories of relativity. The other was Quantum Mechanics.

To begin with, the atom is that microscopic entity once thought to be a small, solid and indestructible particle which made up all matter. Now we find it is really only like a poof of energy, since all matter can be converted into energy.

Early research resulted in the surprising discovery that the atom, small as it is, is actually an expanse of space. In it extremely tiny negative-charge electrons speed around a nucleus, which consists of one or more positive-charge protons and neutral neutrons. The only exception is the most common element, hydrogen, the nucleus of which has only a proton. This all sounds reasonable, that is, until you discover how small small is.

Different authors describe the size of an atom and its parts differently. My favorite is found in *The Tao of Physics* written by Fritjof Capra. He suggests that we imagine an orange represents the atom. Then picture that orange the size of the earth and stuff it with cherries.

That's how many atoms there are in an orange. Remember, each atom has a nucleus consisting of at least one proton and a neutron, and that nucleus is being constantly circled by ever so tiny electrons. How small is the nucleus? Author Capra suggests that if you enlarge the atom to the size of the dome of St. Peter's Cathedral in Rome, the nucleus would be like a grain of salt and the electrons dancing around it like specks of dust. That's small!

Their small size is not the only puzzling characteristic of subatomic entities. You can't describe them merely as particles. Depending on how you view them, that is what kind of equipment is used in the experiments with them, they can take the form of a wave, too.

This dual nature is just as true of light as it is of matter. We speak of light waves and say they travel at 186,000 miles per second, but light can also take the form of particles. We call them photons. Unlike the particles in matter, photons are massless and always travel at the speed of light. I couldn't help wondering if this wave formation is not also true of thoughts. Do these little so-called thotons take the form of waves, too, and how fast do those waves travel?

The more I've learned about Quantum Mechanics the more I find my husband and I thinking the same thing at almost the same time, even when he's thousands of miles away. I've had other experiences recently, too, which suggest that our thoughts are impacted in ways we have never imagined. Just recently I was reading the obituaries in our local paper and was reminded of one of the homebound individuals whom I had visited in her home periodically over several years. The next day I learned she had died just about the time I was thinking of her. Coincidence? I don't think so!

Another useful insight into Quantum Mechanics has to do with how physicists study either the particle or the wave nature of subatomic entities. You can't do both at the same time. It takes one kind of testing equipment for research on wave action and another for particle action. To be precise, the type of testing equipment determines the form of the subatomic entities. This means that the tester decides what form the subatomic entities being studied will take and, therefore, is actually a participant in the process, a part of it and not apart from it.

Back to Newtonian physics now. Remember, it made the space program possible because it enables us to predict where a physical object will go in a specific time if we know its speed. This is not true with subatomic particles. Experiments only show tendencies or probabilities for any single particle. That's because subatomic entities, tested as particles, interact with each other so rapidly that it's not possible to see them and to pinpoint where and what occurs at any specific time. All you can see of them in certain tests are the streaks of light which indicate the energy they create as they dance. Time and space merge together. It's like the whirling blades of a fan moving at top speed. You can feel the breeze that's created but you can't see the blades that create it. This is the essence of relativity. The three dimensions of width, length and depth add the fourth dimension of time-space.

Here is an interesting observation on that note. Is the real you and the real me actually a Dancing Spirit inside our physical bio-body suit? Is it invisible and, if so, why? Could it be because that Dancing Spirit consists of subatomic entities which dance together so rapidly they cannot be seen in circumstances where time and space are separate dimensions? If that's the case in Quantum Mechanics research on subatomic entities, as has been proven, it must be applicable to our Dancing Spirit, too. I can't help but think of those tantalizing comments of St. Paul in his first letter to the church at Corinth.

> *"But some will ask, 'How are the dead raised? With what kind of body do they come?' You foolish man! What you sow does not come to life unless it dies... What is sown is perishable, what is raised is imperishable...It is sown a physical body, it is raised a spiritual body...we shall all be changed..."*
>
> —1 Corinthians 15:35 ff.

The dictionary defines spiritual as "incorporeal" and incorporeal as "having no material body or form." It's almost as if Paul already understood what science is now uncovering.

But let's get back to Quantum Mechanics. What happens to any single particle is determined then by its relationship with other particles. Those tiny subatomic particles might as well be saying, "We're all in this together!" The more research that is done, the more the message comes through that the basic elements, those infinitesimally small subatomic entities, whether exhibiting their particle or wave identity, are linked together as parts of the whole of creation. We often speak of a family, a congregation or even of humanity as a whole. Quantum Mechanics indicates a wholeness, a unity of the entire universe.

This becomes even more obvious when we look a little closer at the atom, especially the very tiny nucleus of the atom. Remember, it contains positive-charged protons and neutral neutrons. These subatomic particles respond to their tight quarters by racing around wildly at a speed of about 40,000 miles per second. Such nuclear activity is a reminder that the constant energy we get from the Sun is a result of nuclear reactions too. This is just one example of the use of Quantum Physics in Astronomy and how it helps us understand not only the unity of what occurs on our earth but in our entire cosmos.

What happens in the world of subatomics actually reflects what happens in the world of stars and galaxies, too. Just as it takes special equipment to study particles and waves, it takes super-powerful telescopes to see our cosmic universe in constant motion. Gases form stars which then throw off material into space which, in turn, can become planets. But let's get back to those speeding little sub-atomic particles or waves.

Thanks to Einstein and his famous formula, $E=MC^2$ or energy equals mass times the speed of light squared, we now know that mass or matter is actually a form of energy. To study how mass or matter becomes energy, huge accelerators have been built which allow physicists to observe the dancing and creation process of subatomic particles. The accelerators cause the particles to move faster and faster. They collide with each other and self-destruct. Well, not exactly. They actually may recreate a replica of themselves and create other tiny particles as well, emitting energy in the process. Some of these new particles, all of which have been given a name, actually may live for only a millionth of a second or even less. They can't even be seen, but the tracks that show where they've been are caught by the camera as streaks of light which are a form of energy. This illustrates the fact that mass is equivalent to a specific amount of energy. Even more fascinating, this means we have to think of mass or matter not as an unchangeable entity but as a process, a work in progress, constantly dancing, constantly changing, actually self-sacrificing as entities bump into each other but creating new entities and seemingly resurrecting themselves, all while giving off energy in the process.

You know what that makes us? Since we are composed of atoms and their sub-atomic parts, which keep on dancing energetically, self-sacrificing and resurrect-ing, we too are a work in progress. Our life is the dance of all those tiny subatomic entities constantly colliding, creating, giving off energy and changing who and what we are and can become. That's true of our physical bio-body, we know. Depending on how we take care of it, it can help us live a happier, more productive physical life. But how about our Spirit? How about those invisible, everlasting entities that dance inside our physical body? What happens when we finally toss aside that worn-out physical bio-body suit? All that is left is pure energy, pure dancing energy, and energy cannot be destroyed. Like sound waves or light waves, and perhaps thought waves, they live eternally.

Over the years of my long life I have read and studied many ways in which people have searched for, believed in and had faith in so many different ways to understand and insure the eternal happiness of their Spirit. Whether we call it Heaven, the Hereafter, Nirvana, Happy Hunting Ground or whatever, we all want the hope and joy of knowing our Spirit will reach it. Even for those who may not believe in it, I feel they must have an unconscious longing for it to exist. A place to meet our loved ones again, a chance to put aside the mistakes we've made, to do it better, to be loved and to love. It sounds almost too good to be true yet believers of major religions have faith that this is true.

As you read about some of those searches and beliefs in different religions in the chapters to come, you'll see for yourself how true that is. Since the dawn of humankind, the need to hope for, the need to believe that the best is yet to come seems to be innate in us. We are born with that need. Is it our invisible, everlasting Spirit encouraging us and, if so, how do we connect with that Spirit and whoever or whatever it came from and to which it returns? Some of us do so through prayer, through meditation, through reaching out in love to those in need. Others do so through science, whether it's the study of the human mind and personality, the physical body or the entire cosmos. And now Quantum Physics appears to be bringing it all together, a signal that perhaps we're all right. We just use different methods to understand and express ourselves and different words to describe the same realities. After all, people all over the earth speak different languages but they do so to express the same needs, the same emotions, the same fears, and the same hopes for joy and fulfillment or, as some call it, justification for our mistakes and salvation for our eternal Spirit.

We are fortunate to live in an era where Quantum Physics and research in the realm of the invisible or spiritual dimension of existence are seemingly "singing off the same song sheet." Which is why, in this chapter on Quantum Physics, I choose to share with you briefly how this complicated subject may help even we scientific neophytes understand how we may actually scientifically help our illusive, invisible Spirit to dance as it never has before.

When I read my first two books on Quantum Mechanics which stressed the apparent relationship between fact and faith, I was overjoyed. Then I began to read further. The internet is a treasure of articles, and the bookstores and libraries are replete with books on the subject. As professional theologians and believers from many religious denominations differ in their spiritual faith, so I found professional physicists and amateurs in the field as well differ in how they view Quantum Physics.

The world's first Quantum Theory was conceived by Werner Heisenberg in the summer of 1925. A Quantum Theory is a way of understanding quantum entities, what attributes they possess, how they go through various actions, and how all this impacts everything in this world. In physics all this must be expressed in mathematical symbols. What the symbols do on paper, the quantum entities do in the world. Later that same year, Erwin Schrödinger produced a different mathematical version of the same underlying theory. Paul Dirac than came up with a theory showing how one could be transformed into the other. All three claimed to explain our world and all three proved to be right.

What is important is not specifically what the three theories were since the subjects are highly technical. What happened is important. Physicists worldwide began to test the new theories against what happens in the world and they set out on two different tracks. The first group used Quantum Theory as a symbolic tool to manipulate the world. The second group used it as a window into reality.

The first group has become known for its Copenhagen interpretation, because it was championed originally and mainly by Niels Bohr, a Danish physicist. The Copenhagen interpretation affirms that there is no deep reality or, simply put, there is no quantum world. There is only what we can observe in specific tests involving quantum entities. If they are not tested, they do not exist. Some physicists take an additional step and maintain that if we don't see them, they just aren't there. It is our consciousness of them which creates them. This reminds one of the old question, "If no one is there to observe the forest, does it exist?" Or, "If no one is there to hear the birds, do they really sing?"

So began differences of opinion which became more complicated and definitive over time. One of the most noted physicists who took exception to Bohr's view of Quantum Theory was Albert Einstein. In 1935 he developed an experiment, with the help of two other physicists, which came to be known as the EPR experiment (the first initial of each of the last names of the three physicists). It did not show that Quantum Theory was invalid but rather that it failed to detect certain elements of reality, that is what Einstein and others understood to be reality, which were not directly observable by Quantum Mechanics. It reinforced

Einstein's belief that Quantum Mechanics was incomplete and stressed the need to find a way to explain all of reality, even that which is not directly observable. That search still continues.

In 1964, some nine years after Einstein's death, John Bell, an Irish physicist from Belfast, devised a proof which he believed resolved the dilemma. This proof came to be known as Bell's Theorem. Critics of Quantum Theory assume that all reality is local, that it involves local interaction or direct contact. Without going into technical explanations, if one views reality as non-local, namely that which may happen without any apparent direct contact, or action at a distance, it would mean that Quantum Theory is valid. To put Bell's Theorem in simple terms, it illustrates that reality is non-local, that what happens in one location may impact what happens in another location, distant and unrelated in time and space, leaving Quantum Theory intact.

Two physicists, John Clauser at Columbia University and Alain Aspect at the University of Paris, did additional work over the next decades which confirmed Bell's conclusions. In fact, it is believed by some physicists that it's possible, in view of their work, Bell's Theorem would still be valid even if Quantum Theory were replaced by other theories.

In spite of all this, many physicists tend to reject Bell's Theorem because they believe it cannot be proven. Some physicians who have done research in the power of prayer to heal disagree. Likewise there are proven instances, both in the sciences and social sciences, of thought transfer tests which impact physical outcome beyond time and space. Report after report like these tend to suggest that Bell's Theorem is correct: Reality is non-local.

On the one hand, many physicists who maintain that reality cannot be reached through Quantum Mechanics pursue other avenues for an overall theory of reality. One of the latest is String Theory, which is not in competition with Quantum Theory but treats subatomic entities as tiny, oscillating lines or loops. On the other hand, there are those for whom Bell's Theorem proves that reality is non-local. If Quantum Mechanics ever does fall by the wayside of research, what happens to Bell's Theorem? Is reality non-local? And, if not, how can I explain why I dreamt my husband was injured when, unknown to me, miles across the Caribbean he was injured as someone reached into his car and jerked off the camera held by a strong cord around his neck? That is only one story I have to tell. There are others I have to share as well.

Helping me to clarify my thinking on the subject of reality being non-local was another book by Gary Zukav, whose first book was *The Dancing Wu Li Masters*. Having concluded in it that there was a definite relationship between ancient

Eastern World religions and science, he went on to write a new book entitled *The Seat of the Soul*. In this new work he shares and expands on that relationship and suggests how we can connect with and encourage our Spirit in its longing for hope and joy now as well as hope for the future. It has been a thought-starter for me in sharing with you my own conclusions.

You may remember someone, or even yourself, refer to having a sixth sense about something. Zukav suggests we are not five-sensory people. We do not just see, hear, smell, feel and taste. We intuit. We sense something is true or false, right or wrong. We have intuitions, messages from our Soul or Spirit, from God, our Guardian Angel, our Spirit Guide, our God-given conscience, or whatever we choose to call that "inner voice." It's like a "letter from home," where we come from and to which we shall return. Our bio-body lives in physical reality with physical senses but our invisible Spirit is our non-physical reality and acts and reacts non-locally. How do we know?

Quantum Physics explains it. We can't see those smaller-than-microscopic entities of which we are composed. All we can see are the streaks of light the camera shows as those little living entities dance in eternal joy. How do we know we truly have valid intuitions? How did I know my husband had his neck scraped red and sore when he was in Haiti and I was in Florida? How did I think of my dying friend when she was half a city away from me and I hadn't seen, spoken to or heard about her for several weeks? Why do I know I must write these words for anyone out there who longs to have hope and joy now in the blessed assurance that the best is yet to come? I just do! Hardly a week passes that some occurrence doesn't make an even firmer believer out of me. The series of seeming coincidences that led me to attempt to write this book as I near the close of my bio-body's 80th year is proof. I should be putting away my dancing shoes and shopping for a walker. Instead, I'm asking you to join me, whether you're eighteen or eighty. Come, let your Spirit dance with mine. Here is a semi-scientific suggestion of how it is possible.

Remember those streaks of light that only the camera sees in Quantum Physics research? That is actually pure energy, visible to us as light. Just as those subatomic entities being researched are systems which create and emit energy so are we, so is our invisible, non-physical Spirit. We, too, send out streaks of energy. That's what emotions are. They are streaks or currents of energy. The negative emotions like fear, hatred, envy, and jealousy have a lower frequency. The positive emotions like sympathy, compassion, kindness and, most of all, love have a higher frequency. The greater the frequency, that is the faster your invisible Spirit dances, the more positive energy flows through you and moves, sometimes instantaneously, to others. And, because such high frequency blends time and space together, the result seems in our physically limited world to be instantaneous or non-local. By just reaching out in kindness, caring and love to someone else, by speaking a word of praise or thank you, your Spirit will dance more energetically and those you touch, even beyond time and space or non-locally, will dance with you.

It sounds fanciful and magical, I know, but our earth, our universe, all seem magical and miraculous. Let me put it in a simple everyday way, one suggested by my ever-patient, always-supportive, always positive and encouraging husband.

We may change form, just like water does. When it's cold, water freezes solid and is immobile. When it warms up a bit, those little subatomic particles move around faster and water becomes liquid. Then when those little dancing particles warm up even more, they dance faster and faster until "Poof," the water becomes a quickly disappearing cloud of steam. How does that apply to us?

Look at it this way. We, too, change our form and we can control that change. When we're anxious and fearful, self-centered and unsympathetic with those around us, lost in our own problems, we're in an emotional rut, out of which we can't seem to move. We're unable to interrelate with others. Like ice, we are practically immobile. When we look around and recognize that others are in need, physical and emotional, and we can perhaps reach out to help, our pace quickens. We begin to move around, emotionally and physically, bump into others, self-sacrifice our own egos and create new circumstances. Like water in its liquid form, we go with the flow.

Then we get to the point where we count our blessings, count them one by one, and in thankfulness reach out wholeheartedly, unselfishly, in love for others. We literally self-sacrifice who we were and begin to create ourself anew. We pick up the pace of life and our Spirit dances faster and better. Like water becomes steam, we are almost like pure energy, exerting a powerful force on all around us.

I like to think that's what happens with us and our worn-out bio-body suit. We realize and accept the fact that our life, our work in progress, is almost completed. Just as the science of physics moved from the Classical to the Quantum stage, we become ready to move to a new dimension. The hope that it will be a new and fulfilling adventure gives us joy indescribable. Our Spirit, a composite of subatomic particles, literally dances with hope and joy.

When finally we're ready to cast off that worn-out bio-body suit, our Spirit dances with a special kind of grace, an expression of God's love for us. We listen to our Spirit Father God and are reminded to love one another. Our willing Spirit almost literally collides in love for others, dancing as it never has before.

Our hope and joy here and for hereafter overwhelm us. Then suddenly,"Poof," we're free-at-last, a Spirit free of time and space, a Spirit rising to meet God unencumbered. We call it "death." It's really "crossing over" to the eternal life of our Dancing Spirit. Knowing and believing this is a special blessing.

Remember my reference a few paragraphs back about the woman whom I thought of while scanning the obituaries in our daily paper? I hadn't thought so pointedly of her for some days and so it was somewhat startling to find she had died at just about the time I was thinking of her. There's more to the story.

For some two and a half years, as volunteer Visitation Minister for our church, I had been calling on and keeping in touch with her and her husband. He had died only months before and she and I had last spoken over the phone a few weeks ago. She was alone and anxious, barely able to see or to breathe easily enough to move around the house, and ever so lonely. Her husband had been a pilot and shared with me privately how difficult it was to be housebound and earthbound as well, and how he yearned to fly again. I shared these stories with her on the phone and commented how wonderful it was he could do that, how his spirit was free now to break the bonds of time and space and fly again. And I added how she was free to let her Spirit dance now in the hope that they would ultimately share the joy of soaring through time and space together.

I can remember her, still hear her asking, "Do you really believe that?" "Oh, yes, I really believe it. I'm sure of it," I replied. It was our last conversation and so, when I heard of her passing, I could only think of the two of them, free at last, free of aching limbs, failing eyes, labored breathing. Free of time and space, free to rise unencumbered, their Dancing Spirits sharing love and joy.

No, I'm not a physicist, not the greatest at understanding the complicated world of subatomics, and certainly not the greatest at explaining it. Nevertheless, it is my firm conviction that the research in Quantum Physics in the last century has done even more than show a relationship between science and ancient Eastern religions. I believe it points to truths in the Western World's religions, including what is popularly known as New Age Spirituality, and especially for those of us who are Christian.

The more I have read, studied and learned about subatomic physics, Quantum Mechanics, the stronger my beliefs have become. Moreover, the longer I have served in the ministry, especially in my associations with individuals facing pain, anxiety, and fear of both life here in our physical world and of the hereafter, the more convinced I have become. Furthermore, the history of world religions and contemporary spirituality reinforce my convictions. Add to that the medical doctors who have researched the power of prayer in healing, the proven record of psychiatrists who successfully use regressive life therapy, the work of gifted individuals who are conduits between the spiritual dimension and our physical world and my own experiences.

Now, top all this with the helpful practice, both physically and spiritually, of meditation or centering prayer, our Christian counterpart to the research of Quantum Mechanics. As physicists conduct tests to reach the reality of our world, we reach deep within to find the reality of our true Spirit.

When you read about all these subjects in the chapters to come, keep in mind the basic points to remember about Quantum Physics, both the scientific facts which indicate we dance because we are truly created to dance and the basic pattern this establishes for all humanity.

1. **The unity of the universe**: No single subatomic entity lives in isolation but only in a dancing relationship with others, even non-locally or faster than the speed of light. This indicates the wholeness and unity of our entire universe, setting the original pattern for humanity to live together on earth and suggesting the reality and unity of the seen and the unseen.

2. **Matter converts to energy and energy cannot be destroyed:** Subatomic particles change form in their dancing relationship with each other, sacrificing themselves and then resurrecting as they give off energy as a streak of light and also create new entities. Just so each of us continually changes who we are as our Spirit lives in a dancing relationship with those around us. We, too, sacrifice our egos as we relate to others, give off energy to them and resurrect ourselves as a new and happier individual. As matter is transformed into energy in the laboratory and that energy can never be destroyed, so we may be transformed, but we can never be destroyed. Our Spirit, which is pure energy, like a streak of light, lives forever. Our faith promises us that and now fact confirms it.

3. **Choices made impact results achieved**: The tester in Quantum Mechanics chooses the equipment used in each test and how it is used. These choices determine whether it is waves or particles which are studied and the resultant actions of those entities. Just so each of us chooses how we use the abilities and characteristics with which we have been blessed and those choices help to form the person we become. The individual is part of the process in science and life and thus impacts results achieved. The tester is a part of the test and not apart from it.

4. **The truth is found deep within**: Quantum Mechanics discovered the ever-lasting basic dancing entities of life by research at greater depths than ever thought possible. Just so humans meditate and pray, reaching deep within to find the truth that each of us is indeed an everlasting Dancing Spirit, created to live in dancing relationships with others. Scientific research reveals the streaks of light which signify the energy of life. People of faith open hearts and minds to God in centering prayer and hear God's Spirit whom Christians, for example, have come to know through the words and deeds of Jesus, God's Christ. The facts of science found in deepest research provide a new paradigm for faith in the everlasting energy of life.

On these basic conclusions, based on my study of Quantum Mechanics and the major religions of the world as well as contemporary spirituality, this is my theory:

> **Science and religion have joined together to reassure us in our Christian faith...to encourage us to listen to God's Spirit within us...and to help our own invisible Spirit dance in loving relationships and so find hope and joy both for here and hereafter.**

Read now, with open mind and open heart, to review the age-old history of humanity's search for God and immortality and the latest history of humanity's scientific discoveries. They are, in my convictions, a view of reality from different perspectives. They are fact and faith joined together. They are reassurance that life is a dance of the invisible essence of our own true Spirit. As we make choices to live together in mutual concern, care and love, our Spirit will dance in hope and joy both here and hereafter.

Come, dance with me!

3

The East Dances First

The Dancing God Shiva is an ancient Hindu Symbol.
He illustrates creation, preservation, destruction, embodiment
and release of the Spirit from the illusion of life and the
way to spiritual enlightment and true wisdom.

—Dharam Vir Singh
Hinduism, An Introduction[1]

Hinduism, the oldest of Eastern World religions, embraces dancing in a religious symbol. The Hindu God Shiva, known as the Dancing God, dances perpetually, representing continual destruction and creation in the endless rhythm of the universe.[2]

The roots of Hinduism may stretch back to the misty past between the fifth and third millennia B.C.E. (Before the Christian Era). Evidence indicates the existence of a people known as the Tumi Culture living in the regions north of the Black Sea between the Carpathian Mountains and the Caucasus. Their origins are rooted in Neolithic times, perhaps even earlier.

Over the centuries they migrated in three different directions. Some went into central and northern Europe, others south into the Mediterranean and Middle East where they contributed to some of the religions of the Western World, and finally some went east into India. They came to be known as Indo-Europeans or, as they called themselves, Aryans which comes from the Sanskrit language. It means "noble men." Some of their earliest beliefs and practices were incorporated into what we now know as Hinduism.[3]

For example, there were figures of a male god with three faces or three ways of seeing god, just as in the Christian Trinity we have three ways of understanding and relating to God. This triune god was probably later expressed by the three Hindu gods, Brahma, Vishnu or Krishna, and Shiva, the dancing god.[4]

21

It was around the middle of the second millennium B.C.E. that these tall, light-skinned Aryans invaded India. Unfortunately, there are no archeological finds from the early Aryan settlements but there are manuscripts written down around 800 B.C.E. Since they are written in a much more ancient language, they may have been composed long before these people came to India and were thus part of an early oral tradition.[5] The earliest of these writings is known as the Rig Veda or "songs of knowledge." It is a collection of hymns of praise, often addressed to a single god, similar to the Psalms in our Bible.

As in Christianity, sacrifice is also a recurring theme in Hinduism, as was illustrated in one of its important rituals. It stresses that there can be no life without sacrifice and reminds one of both science and religion.[6] On one hand, we think of the subatomic particles in Quantum Physics in their continual dance of self-sacrifice, only to reappear and create new life. On the other hand, it resonates with the Christian ritual of the Mass or Holy Communion, which recognizes God's sacrifice so that humanity can have new life. All suggest an ongoing and everlasting unity of the universe.

At the time of the sacrifice, one priest, known as the hotar or libation-pourer, would set out on the grass the items used in the rite. They were cake and Soma, which was an intoxicating liquid. Then he would chant his invitation to the participants who would eat and drink of the cake and Soma, chanting a prayer as they finished.

Throughout the centuries major changes took place[7] as the beliefs and practices of modern Hinduism evolved. One major area is the concentration on devotion as a means of finding what is often called salvation but may also be described as fulfillment or eternal peace.[8]

It was the way of devotion which ultimately led to the writing of the famous *Bhagavad-Gita* or Song of the Blessed Lord, a classic of religious literature. Composed over a period of eight hundred years (400 B.C.E. to 400 A.D.), it contains one hundred thousand couplets, has influenced Hinduism for nearly two thousand years, and has won many converts to Hinduism.[9]

Remember the three-faced god of the early Indians. We meet them now in the *Bhagavad-Gita* as Brahma, the World-Spirit to whom all would one day return, Shiva and Krishna. True reality or the ground of being is called Brahman, and a description of Brahman sounds much like Christians try to describe God the Father, Son and Holy Spirit. Indians, wishing to talk about and describe Brahman, have simply created many gods, each of which exemplifies some characteristic of the indescribable Brahman. They are not gods but simply reflections of the one true reality. Brahman himself is the totality of all the gods. Further, they believe reality or Brahman is part of every person and gives that essence the name Atman. Just so Christians believe that the Holy Spirit is always inherent in us all. The idea that Atman and Brahman, the individual and the god, are one is the essence of the *Upanishads*.[10]

Once again we have a sensing of science and religion coming together. Brahman and Atman, representing individuals and all of ultimate reality, suggest the unity of the universe, just as Quantum Physics does. At the same time, Atman as the essence of Brahman in each individual sounds much like a description of the Holy Spirit, the essence of God in each of us. Then there is the devotion to those many Indian gods, simply symbols of the many faces of reality, which reminds us of the devotion of many Christians to the saints.

One last dramatic story from the *Bhagavad-Gita* which I would like to share with you is that of the god Krishna appearing as a charioteer for a warrior. Krishna tells the warrior:

> I am the Sacrifice! I am the Prayer!
> I am the Funeral-cake set for the dead!…cling thou to Me!
> Clasp Me with heart and mind! So shalt thou dwell
> Surely with me on high…
> Give Me thy heart! adore Me! serve Me! cling
> In faith and love and reverence to Me
> So shalt thou come to Me! I promise true.
> Make Me thy single refuge! I will free
> Thy soul from all its sins! Be of good cheer! [11]

The words of Krishna to the warrior could have been spoken by Jesus to each Christian struggling as a warrior in the battle of life. And again, we are reminded of those subatomic particles which sacrifice self only to resurrect, create new entities and give off life-enhancing energy.

That brings us to two of the major beliefs of Hinduism, karma and reincarnation. Karma, which is the law of actions, simply means that every good thought, word or deed results in a similar action which impacts our next lives. Likewise, every unkind or selfish thought, word or deed will come back to plague us in this life and the next. That is karma. The best or ideal karma is that which is performed as a point of duty towards god or humankind, without looking for any personal rewards. The next step, of course, is reincarnation. Hinduism accepts as a matter of fact that our Spirit sheds its earthly body and returns to a spiritual dimension, only to return to earth again and again as a new person. Once again, their beliefs suggest the unity of the universe, the ongoing and everlasting creation and transformation of all that is, seen and unseen.

Religion and science come together. Religion fills the needs of humanity. Quantum Physics verifies that such fulfillment is a reflection of the actions of the basic matter and energy of life. Hinduism foreshadows later religious developments, even in Christianity, and now Quantum Physics puts on its stamp of approval.

◆   ◆   ◆

The realms of all sentient beings
Whirl in the sea of birth and death.
Buddha emits a pain-killing light:
The unhindered spirit can see this.
Avatamsaka Sutra[12]

Buddhism has for many centuries been the major religion of Asia as Hinduism has been for India. Actually, as Christianity grew out of Judaism in the western hemisphere, so Buddhism grew out of Hinduism in the East. As Hindus use the symbol of the Dancing God Shiva to indicate the ongoing dance of life, so Buddhists use the symbol of the wheel of life to illustrate the world in which we live. They, too, believe that we create our own karma which determines the nature of our ongoing lives. To escape from the pain and suffering of this world, however, was the objective of the Buddha,[13] and the Spirit could find that escape.

Buddha was born in 566 B.C.E. in a village near the modern border between India and Nepal. His name was Siddharta Gautama and his father was a wealthy rajah. Determined to insure a good life for his son, Siddharta's father surrounded his son with luxury, gave him an excellent education, and shielded him from the pain and ugliness of the outside world. Though he lived in the midst of luxury, he was discontent and found no satisfaction in his life.[14]

As a result, when he was a young man, he shaved his head, donned the rough yellow robe of a wandering mendicant and left home. Shocked by the misery, poverty and death he witnessed in the world, Siddharta was determined to search for a way to escape the endless cycle of rebirth which was the general belief in his Hindu background.[15]

After some six years of yoga training and subjecting his body to starvation and asceticism, he concluded that he had not found the answers for which he searched. Relaxing under the shade of a tree and letting his thoughts roam, the answer came to him. From that time on, he was known as the Buddha, which means "the enlightened one." The answer, he believed, was to detach oneself, to enter a new state of human consciousness which came to be known as Nirvana.[16]

The word Nirvana comes from a verb which means "to waft away." It is a condition where desire ends, a turning away from sensuality, selfishness, and excesses of any kind.[17] In other words, the Buddha advocated self-sacrifice of one's own ego, of catering to the physical desires of the body and personality. He stressed letting go of hatred and ignorance, advocating the middle way between materialism and idealism. As Quantum Physics illustrates self-sacrifice of the basic entities in the subatomic world, leading to resurrection and new creation, so the way of the Buddha also taught a constant self-sacrifice and resurrecting of one's self.

On the subject of the unity of all that is, Buddha took a step beyond Hinduism. His goal was to eventually stop the endless wheel of reincarnation from life after life and in that way to achieve ultimate and complete Nirvana. He therefore rejected the idea of a separate and individual soul or spirit, believing that all spirits may eventually be reunited with their source or god, as most religions call that source.[18] In Buddhism that source is known as Dharmakaya and can best be described as that ultimate indivisible reality of which all things are a part. In Hinduism it is Brahman. In Quantum Physics that unity is stressed by the fact that subatomic entities cannot be studied in isolation but only in their interrelatedness.[19]

Meditation was the way in which the Buddha ultimately found the enlightenment which is the foundation of Buddhist beliefs. When all else failed, he sat under a tree and turned off his mind to reach a spiritual depth just as we, in centering prayer, wait for God to talk with us. This is precisely what the Buddha did, and the answers he received were much the same as those stressed in Hinduism and in Christianity, as the following quotation reveals.

> To do no evil; To cultivate good; To purify one's mind:
> This is the teaching of the Buddhas.[20]

The image of Buddha in meditation is as significant to Buddhists as the figure of Christ on the cross is to Christians. As Buddha committed himself and ultimately his followers to sacrifice body and personality desires to reach Nirvana so Christ sacrificed himself so that all, by following and believing in him, could achieve what we Christians refer to as heaven or salvation.[21] Since Buddha did not stress Dharmakaya or the ultimate indivisible reality as an individual god, in the same sense as Hindus regard Brahman, prayer was not a practice he advocated. After his death, however, his followers turned the discipline of meditation into prayer to the Buddha, much as Christians pray to Jesus.[22] In fact, throughout the eastern part of the world, Buddhists use prayer wheels and beads, much like Hindu prayer beads and the Christian rosary.

Dance, too, is a ritual of the Buddhist monks. In Korea the "Sungmu" or Monk's Dance is a coming together of color, music and movement. It depicts the emotions of a monk torn between the monastic and mundane worlds. Two common ritual dances in praise of the Buddha are the Butterfly Dance and the Cymbals Dance, traditionally performed in a temple compound. [23]

One final belief in Buddhism almost seems to foretell the latest scientific research results. It is the Buddhist concept of dharmas. Dharmas are considered to be the ultimate elements or particles of the universe. Like atoms, they are very tiny and exist only for a split second. They are described as flashes of colored light and can be likened to the flashes of light which are the evidence Quantum Physics has to prove the existence of subatomic entities.

Ancient Buddhas believed that these dharmas make up the four basic elements: earth, water, air and fire. And ultimately they believe all "things" are nothing more than bundles of these qualities or actions. The word quantum means bundle, a bundle of subatomic entities which constantly are in action, literally dancing, as they emit energy.[24] It's as though the ancient Buddhists had already discovered what Quantum Physics is now illustrating.

◆   ◆   ◆

The way is gained by daily loss,
Loss upon loss until
At last comes rest…
The world is won by those who let it go!
Tao Te Ching, Verse 48

Taoism and **Confucianism**, the major religions of China, developed against the background of much older religious beliefs, just as Buddhism developed against the background of Hinduism in India.

Ancient China was an agricultural civilization and worship of the earth with emphasis on planting, harvesting, and fertility was a major part of the culture. By the mid-second millennium B.C.E., however, there is evidence of worship of heaven as well. Also, a god was worshipped whose name was Shang Ti, which means "upper ruler." Shang Ti had no clearly defined personality and did not communicate directly with humans as our Christian God in the Hebrew Scriptures did. Rather, one learned the thoughts of Shang Ti through divination or trying to decipher various signs in nature.[25]

Ancient Chinese believed in all types of spirits, too, just as Hindus have many gods which represent qualities of Brahman. For the Chinese there were spirits of the earth and of heaven, some of them good and some bad. The people also worshipped their ancestors and there was a kind of interdependency between the dead and the living.[26]

Probably around 1100 B.C.E. some Chinese, whose names we don't know, advanced a new theory. They believed there were two interacting kinds of energy in every natural object, yang and yin. Yang is masculine in character, active, warm, dry, bright, positive, like heaven. Yin is female, fertile, dark, wet, mysterious, negative, like earth. Every object possessed both kinds of energy, though one might remain dormant. When a person died, the spirit, which is yang, joins the ancestral spirits. The body, which is yin, sinks to the earth and disintegrates.[27]

The ancient Chinese had a theory to explain the harmony and order in nature, too. They called it the Tao, which means "way" or "road." The Tao of the universe was believed to be eternal, existing even before the world. According to this preordained Tao, the physical world came to be. As long as the world and all in it followed the Tao, heaven, earth and humans would form a single, harmonious unit.[28]

In other words, Tao was the original, the ultimate, indefinable reality, like the Hindu Brahman, the Buddhist Dharmakaya or our Christian God. It also goes beyond them in that it is seen as the cosmic process in which all creation is involved as a continuous flow and change, like the ongoing dance of the subatomic particles in Quantum Physics.[29]

Comparing Taoism to other religions brings up another interesting similarity. Like Hinduism and Christianity, the ancient Chinese also had a triune god to whom they paid highest honors. They were T'ai I, the ultimate oneness…T'ien I, heaven…and Ti I, earth.[30]

It was against the background of all these beliefs that both Confucianism and Taoism developed, the first emphasizing human relations, the second the workings of nature. We might compare them to Confucianism as the Christian concept of Law, which we know in the Ten Commandments, and Taoism as Gospel, which we know through Jesus. The latter we cannot come to know through the intellect but must accept by faith. Just so, Taoism is based on the belief that one can never understand life and our world through the intellect but one must probe deeper than the mind. As such it is more like Hinduism and Buddhism and, yes, like Quantum Physics which studies the unseen, the mysterious subatomic entities. And so it is into Taoism we shall probe with intellect and, hopefully, from a spiritual perspective as well.

Mystery shrouds the beginnings of Taoism, though some say it was Lao Tzu, born around 604 B.C.E., who began it all. The name means "Old Master." Legend has it that Lao Tzu wrote down his beliefs in the *Tao Te Ching* before disappearing through a mountain pass. More authoritative scholarship suggests the work was written much later by more than one author. [31]

A second important book in Taoism is the *Chuang-tzu*. The author, Chuang-tzu, is believed to have lived about two hundred years after Lao Tzu. Like the *Tao Te Ching*, the *Chuang-tzu* is also believed to have been written by different authors at different times.[32]

Whenever or by whomever they were written, both the *Tao Te Ching* and *Chuang-tzu* have ideas that are hauntingly like the writings of other religions. For example, there is verse 48 from the *Tao Te Ching* quoted at the beginning of this section which stresses the need for daily loss or self-sacrifice for those who seek ultimate rest or true fulfillment. Also on the subject of self-sacrifice or selflessness, there is verse 7 of the *Tao Te Ching*:

> The Wise Man chooses to be last
> And so becomes the first of all;
> Denying self, he too is saved.
> For does he not fulfillment find
> In being an unselfish man?

It sounds like the Taoist version of Jesus' words centuries later.

"If anyone would be first, he must be last of all and servant of all."
—The Bible, Mark 9:35

Like the other ancient Eastern religions, Taoism believes in the unity of all reality. To quote a dedicated scholar of Chinese culture, R. B. Blakney, "Reality, however designated is One; it is an all-embracing unity from which nothing can be separated."[33] As an example, he quotes verse 25 of the *Tao Te Ching*:

> Something there is, whose veiled creation was
> Before the earth or sky began to be;
> So silent, so aloof and so alone
> It changes not, nor fails, but touches all.

To take that concept of unity to all of humankind, Blakney quotes verse 47:[34]

> The world may be known
> Without leaving the house;
> The Tao may be seen
> Apart from the windows.
> The farther you go,
> The less you will know.

To make contact with inner reality, one needs to listen to the Spirit of God within us.

All this ancient wisdom suggests that the Tao illustrates the importance of self-sacrifice or selflessness, the unity of all reality and the way to reach that reality within one is through centering prayer. One significant question remains for us to ask, "Do the Taoists dance?" Again, to put it in the words of the Chinese scholar, R. B. Blakney, "…the Tao (or Way) of nature…is process and not static. The Tao is not a path which nature might take, but is the movement of nature itself; it is an effortless movement…like the annual rhythm of the seasons."[35] The answer is yes, the Tao is in a timeless rhythmic dance!

◆   ◆   ◆

Fact and Faith Come Together: As we compare the four basic conclusions reached in a review of Quantum Physics research with the three major Eastern religions, the similarities are striking. As the subatomic entities of life engage in their invisible dance in scientific research, so Eastern religions present the same basic paradigms for life, namely:

1. The unity of the universe.

2. Matter converts to energy and energy cannot be destroyed.

3. Choices made impact results achieved.

4. The truth is found deep within.

1. The unity of the universe: No single subatomic entity lives in isolation but only in a dancing relationship with others, even non-locally or faster than the speed of light.

> **Hinduism** acknowledges that Brahman is the essence of all reality and is present in each human, illustrating the unity of all that is…and the God Shiva illustrates through his dance the ongoing rhythm of the entire universe.
>
> **Buddhism** takes the unity of the universe even beyond Hinduism in the belief that the ultimate goal is to blend into Dharmakaya or ultimate indivisible reality.
>
> **Taoism** has as its central belief the unity of all reality, described like this by Chinese scholar R. B. Blakney: "The Tao is the Way of ultimate reality. Reality…is one; it is an all-embracing unity from which nothing can be separated."[36]

2. Matter converts to energy and energy cannot be destroyed: Subatomic particles change form in their dancing relationship with each other, sacrificing themselves, then resurrecting as they give off energy as light, an energy which cannot be destroyed.

> **Hinduism** stresses that sacrifice creates the energy of life and it cannot be destroyed. The belief in reincarnation formalizes this aspect of Hindu faith that life is constantly transformed but never destroyed.
>
> **Buddhism** takes the belief of the energy of life being everlasting even further. Buddhists strive to forego the needs and desires of physical life and thus be enabled to merge forever with Dharmakaya, which is all of reality, and thus never be destroyed. This ongoing activity is symbolized by their wheel of life.
>
> **Taoism** teaches that "The world is won by those who let it go!" The Tao or way of life is a positive self-sacrificial relationship with others, which leads to ultimate fulfillment that is everlasting and cannot be destroyed.

3. Choices made impact results achieved: Choices made by the tester in Quantum Physics determine how waves or particles will be studied and, thus, the results that may be achieved. Just so we use our abilities and characteristics to make choices which help to form the person we become.

Hinduism accepts that choices made as individuals interrelate with each other determine both karma and reincarnation, thus impacting not only current life but all future lives as well.

Buddhism carries over belief in karma and reincarnation from Hinduism. As choices made determine karma, so karma determines reincarnation in a future life and ultimate reunion with Dharmakaya.

Taoism acknowledges that the Tao or Way of all reality is a constantly moving, eternally changing dance, and how one follows the Tao determines the harmony and fulfillment which is achieved.

4. The truth is found deep within: Quantum Physics discovered the basic dancing entities of life by research at greater depths than ever thought possible. Just so humans meditate and pray, reaching deep within for the truth, the encouragement and the reassurance that each of us is truly a Dancing Spirit living in relationship with all others.

Hinduism advocates meditation, just as Christians are encouraged to use centering prayer, to touch the reality of the Spirit deep within each of us. As Quantum Physics research reveals the energy of light created by the invisible dance of subatomic entities, so Hindus gain energy and inspiration from the depths of their spiritual center.

Buddhism, like Hinduism, uses meditation to reach the depths of the spirit center and become "enlightened" or united with the essence of all reality. Only through deep meditation can they hope to follow the example of the Buddha and reach Nirvana, just as Christians pray and follow Jesus.

Taoism advocates meditation to contact the inner reality of the invisible spiritual world also. In this way, Taoists believe they will be enabled to join in the effortless ongoing movement of the Tao and come to know the fulfillment which that brings.

4

The West Dances Too

*"Let them praise his name with dancing, making melody
to him with timbrel and lyre!"*

—Psalms 149:3

*"Praise him with timbrel and dance; praise him
with strings and pipe!"*

—Psalms 150:4

Judaism, the oldest of the three major religions of the Western World, endorsed dancing as a means of religious expression from early on.[1] There is ample evidence, however, that the practice of religious dancing was part of what was probably passed down to the Israelites, as they were known, from earlier cultures.

The earliest books of the Hebrew Scriptures, known by Christians as the Old Testament, cover the time before Abraham, considered to be the Father of Judaism. They are actually taken from different ages and from different religious traditions, all put together by later authors probably around the tenth century B.C.E.[2]

For example, the creation story in the second chapter of the book of Genesis indicates man was formed from the earth. This is the same theme found in the Sumerian religion, which flourished in the valley of the Tigris and Euphrates Rivers long before Abraham's time. It was also documented amongst many other primitive people.[3] The Garden of Eden is similar to the original paradise found in other religions as well.[4] The Valley of the Tigris and Euphrates is even suggested as the location of the Biblical Garden of Eden. Sumerians also had a flood myth, and the writers of the Hebrew Scriptures may have known of it. It's possible, too, that both may have picked up the story from an even more ancient religious myth.[5]

It isn't until the time of Abraham that modern authors actually begin the unique history of Israel and the Judaic religion. Abram, who was later to be known as Abraham, was born in approximately 2160 B.C.E. His birthplace was the city of Ur, which is just north of where the Tigris and Euphrates Rivers come together. His father was Terah and Abram was considered to be a descendant in the ninth generation of Shem, the son of Noah.[6] It is believed Abram's family originally came from Akkadia, just north of Sumeria, and that he probably spoke Akkakdian and knew the gods by their Akkadian names. The Akkadian language family includes Hebrew as well as Arabic and Aramaic.

Little is known about the role of dancing in the religions of Akkadians and Sumerians. There is reference to religious dancing in ancient Egypt, however, and the Egyptians are known to have had temple dancers. Since Egyptian religious customs also were known to have influenced the Sumerians, it is reasonable to conclude religious dancing may have been an Akkadian and a Sumerian custom as well.

According to Hebrew Scriptures, Abram moved from the city of Ur to Haran, then via Canaan to Egypt because of a famine, returning ultimately to Canaan. When he was ninety-nine and Sarai, his wife, eighty, God appeared to Abram, changed his name to Abraham and Sarai's to Sarah and promised them a son. The promise was fulfilled. It was their grandson Jacob, later renamed Israel, whose twelve sons made up the tribes of the Israeli nation.

Jacob, known as Israel, moved his family to Egypt around the eighteenth or seventeenth century B.C.E.[7] because of a famine in their homeland. His descendants were ultimately forced into slavery in Egypt, and it was into this environment Moses was born, probably in the thirteenth century B.C.E. There appears to be no doubt that Moses was a real person but myth and mystery surround his early years. His name is of Egyptian derivation, and he was raised by a daughter of the Pharaoh. Being exposed to Egyptian religion, he probably was familiar with the reform which had taken place a century and a half earlier. It was then that the cult of Amon and many gods was replaced with the one god Aton. Aton was believed to have created everything that existed and worship of him included living by a set of rules. This can only bring to mind the one Israelite God, later referred to as Yahweh, and the Ten Commandments which Moses would soon introduce to his people.[8]

Moses's introduction to the role of prophet happened when God's voice came to him and announced that he was to lead God's people out of Egypt to the promised land.[9] Moses did just that, but the people wandered in the desert for some forty years first.

Actually Moses himself was not to enter the land promised by God to the children of Israel. He died just as they approached it, but forever after he has been known for his intimate talks with God and for taking God's word to the people.[10]

Meanwhile, the homeland of Israel's family was known as Canaan from about 1800 to 1200 B.C.E. and, by the time the people arrived from Egypt, many changes had taken place there. The area between Mesopotamia, where Abraham had been born, and Egypt, which the Israelis had left, was populated by many ancient people who are mentioned in the Hebrew Bible. There were the Canaanites, Hittites, Philistines, Edomites, Moabites, Amorites and others as well. Evidence of their civilizations goes back to about 3000 B.C.E.

Between the time the Israelites entered Canaan, around 1200 B.C.E., and proclaimed their first king in 1020 B.C.E., other tribes, impressed by Israeli military victories, also accepted their God, known as Yahweh. Originally Yahweh was a god in the council of the Canaanite supreme god El; but scripture reveals that Yahweh assumed the powers and attributes of El. In the older English translation of Hebrew Scripture, Yahweh is translated as Jehovah.

There were other religious changes, too, as the Israelis adopted some of the customs of the people they conquered. Sanctuaries and sacred sites which previously belonged to El, the major Canaanite god, were consecrated to Yahweh. There seemed to be some confusion, too, between Yahweh and another Canaanite god, Baal. It is possible that originally Baal was accepted along with Yahweh but later rejected.[11] An order of priests developed after the Canaanite models, and even the prophets who began to react against the priests were the product of Canaanite influence.[12]

During the early years of conquest in Canaan, Israel's various tribes were ruled by judges, but pressure mounted to appoint a king. With Yahweh's blessing, Saul was anointed king of Israel. David followed Saul as king and, judging from our opening verses from the book of Psalms, dancing was the ultimate way to praise and thank God. Solomon followed David as king and it was he who built the temple at Jerusalem, which then was considered to be God's home. Even more strongly now, royalty and religion were closely entwined.[13]

This closeness did not exclude influence from Canaanite practices though. Solomon accepted the religions of his wives and sanctuaries were built for their gods. At Solomon's death, the kingdom split in two. Judah in the south had Jerusalem and the temple at its heart while Israel in the north built two sanctuaries, where Yahweh was worshiped as two golden calves.[14]

During the centuries that followed, both countries were besieged by enemies, Israel being taken over by Assyria around 720 B.C.E.[15] Judah faced a similar fate with Jerusalem being destroyed and many people taken to Babylon in 586 B.C.E. Adversity only strengthened religion. Then, as now, people were more inclined to turn to God in time of trouble. Unable to worship in God's house in Jerusalem, the scattered people set up synagogues where worship was held but where there were no sacrifices as had been in the Jerusalem temple. Eventually, the priests were allowed to return to Jerusalem, but it was a different city and strict regulations separated Judean from non-Judean. The first scribes, forerunners of today's rabbis, began to appear. Their work was to interpret the Torah, the book of rules which governed Judaism.[16]

Beginning in 333 B.C.E. with the conquests of Alexander the Great, Greek influence began to be felt. Greek became the spoken language for many Jews in Jerusalem but many, and especially those still in Babylon, spoke Aramaic. The priests remained in power in Jerusalem not only in religious matters but politically and economically as well.[17] And there was continual conflict amongst the people, not only between rich and poor but between those for and those against the Greek way of life.

The question arises here as to whether ancient Greek religious myths had any impact on the Jewish people, as did the Greek language. Like much of the population in areas surrounding the Israelites, the people of Greece and Asia Minor held a common belief in a group of gods known as the Olympians. Most of the myths are from the period of Classical Greece, around 500 B.C.E., but actually are from a much earlier time and had been passed down orally.

In spite of the fact that Greek became the spoken language of many Jews, especially in Jerusalem, little Greek influence in religion seems to be apparent. Also, while Greek may have been the language of state and politics, Aramaic was the language of the people.

On the subject of dancing, it is interesting to note that the early Greeks had perfected the art of dancing into a system which expressed all different passions. One of the earliest records of dancing is by Homer in the *Iliad*. The Hebrew Scriptures or Old Testament used fifty-four different words for dancing, only one of which is a possible reference to secular movement as distinct from religious dancing. As for dancing in modern Judaism, who can deny the spiritual stimulus of dancing the Hora at a Jewish wedding or remain motionless when listening to a tavernful of frolicking men toasting "L'Chaim" (To Life) from *Fiddler on the Roof*?

Following the Greeks, however, there was a new influence from the outside world on the horizon. By early in the second century B.C.E. Rome began moving eastward and, ultimately, the Jewish people were ruled by Rome. Like the Greeks, Romans worshiped a group of gods, very much like the Greek Olympians but with a change in their names. It was similar to what had occurred centuries earlier when the Akkadians in Mesopotamia moved south and joined Sumeria. Together they eventually established the kingdom of Babylonia and, while their gods remained somewhat the same, the names of the gods were changed.

The Roman takeover of the Judaic lands was far more drastic for the people than the Greek conquest had been. It was during these years, when Jews were subjected to religious persecution and many were taken prisoner or fled to other countries, that the Jews' hope for a Messiah, a king of David's line, flourished.[18] This hope paved the way for Jesus to be recognized as Christ, the anointed one of Yahweh, ancient Israel's one God. And it reminds us that, ever since prehistoric times, humans in need of meaning and purpose of life have yearned for a relationship with some source of comfort, love, peace and hope for the future.

The birth of Jesus of Nazareth in no way marked the end of Judaism. Contrarily, as God had promised Abraham and reinforced with Moses, the descendants of Abraham increased and prospered. Due to wars, persecutions, pogroms and holocaust, they dispersed throughout the world in what originally was known as the Diaspora. As a result, over the centuries they have enriched civilizations worldwide, as well as in their homeland, with energy, creativity, intelligence and dedication to social service.

While many Jewish people today may not be actively religious, most do celebrate the Holy or Festival days and seasons from a cultural perspective. Even more significant is that Jewish people are bound together by their common heritage. This gives them a unity and commitment to life which is unique. Judaism truly does reflect the paradigm set by Quantum Mechanics of unity, energy which cannot be destroyed, actions which determine outcome and inspiration and motivation from deep within.

◆   ◆   ◆

I danced in the morning when the world was begun,
And I danced in the moon and the stars and the sun,

And I came down from heaven and I danced on the earth.
At Bethlehem I had my birth.

Dance, then, wherever you may,
I am the Lord of the Dance, said he,
And I'll lead you all, wherever you may be,
And I'll lead you all in the Dance, said he.

Lord of the Dance
Sydney Carter[19]

Christianity today is not considered a "dancing" religion in the more conservative forms of either Catholicism or Protestantism. Of course, there are some congregations with roots in other than conservative European cultures who do express praise, thanksgiving and prayer in physical activities. Perhaps no hymn, of all that have come down to us from the ages or written in our time, however, captures more effectively the life and teachings of Jesus of Nazareth than *Lord of the Dance* written by Sydney Carter in 1963.

To quote Carter, his explanation of how he visualizes Jesus suggests Christianity and Quantum Physics entwined in a dancing song. "I see Christ as the incarnation of the piper who is calling us. He dances that shape and pattern which is at the heart of our reality." Was Jesus a first century prophet suggesting the scientific reality that we are all a "Dancing Spirit?"

Christianity, like all religions, grew from the need of a people to find meaning and comfort in a time of trouble. It was into this kind of world that Jesus was born. The background begins centuries before. After the death of Solomon who had built the great temple in Jerusalem, two Jewish states existed since the people could not agree on one king. The northern state of Israel was conquered by Assyria in 720 B.C.E. and southern Judah by Babylon in 586 B.C.E.

In the early third century B.C.E. the Greeks came and impacted not only the culture of the Jewish people but even the language. After the Greeks came the more barbaric Romans. What could the Jewish hierarchy do then but cooperate with the occupiers? It was the only way for them and the life of the Temple to survive. The people suffered, persecuted on one side by the Romans and on the other by their own religious and political hierarchy. They longed for the Messiah who was promised by their Hebrew prophets.

Exactly when and how Jesus arrived is shrouded in mystery and myth. To those of us who are Christians, the story is graced with fantasy and seen through eyes of faith. No matter that Zoroaster in far eastern Persia (Iran) was believed to have been born of a virgin more than five hundred years or more earlier, or that he was serenaded by a chorus of angels, died, arose and promised to return again. No matter that earlier religions, like the Akkadians and Sumerians, had a trinity God or a life hereafter. Jesus was the salvation of a wounded world in the first century and remains so for countless Christians around the world today.

Having grown up on the stories of Jesus as fashioned by organized religion, I never fully understood the impact Jesus of Nazareth and his message must have had on the troubled people of his time and place. It wasn't until I visited Israel in the early 1990's and was struck by the surrounding desert area and the fact that Israelites then, like Israelies now, longed for peace and freedom. Jesus of Nazareth and his life and message must have been like food and water to an emotionally and physically starved and parched people.

Little is known of Jesus' early life until he was about thirty years old. Then he was baptized by his cousin John, a roving preacher who urged repentance and baptism for the forgiveness of sins. Baptism, incidentally, was already practiced in Judaism and was not unique to Christians. Even then, as in ancient Egypt, new life was signified as rising from the water.

Jesus did, indeed, do just that. He walked out of the Jordan River after being baptized to spend the remainder of his life in preaching and living love and justice. He healed the sick, fed the hungry, championed the poor, the outcasts and those who were on the fringes of society and unacceptable to the Jewish elite. On religious questions, he spoke up against empty ritual and called for more loving relationships with others and with God, whom he called Father.

So popular was he with the common people that Jewish zealots, who wished to incite riot against Roman authorities, were tempted to use him as their champion. They wanted him as a military messiah who would free Israel from Roman rule. The religious elite, not wanting to risk this, collaborated to have him turned over to the Roman authorities.

Ironically, though he refused to be used in the political struggle, he was crucified as "King of the Jews."

As it ultimately turned out, Jesus of Nazareth came to be regarded as far more significant than "King of the Jews." By forty years after Jesus' death, resurrection and beyond, thanks particularly to the Apostle Paul, Jesus became known as Savior of all humanity. To be included in Jesus' gift of eternal salvation, it was necessary to believe that Jesus had died "for our sins." Paul also preached that converts must have the same self-sacrificing attitude as Jesus.[20]

Thus it was Paul, the earliest Christian writer, who created the basic concepts of the religion we know as Christianity.[21] And it was Paul and those who assisted him who carried these concepts to the far reaches of the ancient world. The book of Acts and the epistles of Paul in the Christian New Testament tell the story of how early Christianity was spread.

To totally understand how Christianity developed, however, it is important to note that there was no official Christian doctrine in the early centuries.[22] For example, there were no detailed theories about the crucifixion as atonement for the "original sin" of Adam. This theology did not emerge and develop completely until the fourth century.[23] In fact, it wasn't until the turbulent events of the fourth and fifth centuries that a definition of orthodox Christian belief was worked out and, then, only after an agonizing struggle.

To begin with, at the close of the first century, when the book of Acts was probably completed,[24] most Christians thought about God and prayed to God like Jews. They argued like Rabbis and their churches were like synagogues. In the Roman empire Christianity was seen as a branch of Judaism. As Christianity expanded though, their insistence that theirs was the only God and that all other deities were delusions became a problem.[25] Roman authorities feared that Christians would endanger the state and overturn the fragile order of society.[26]

As time passed more pagans educated in Greco-Roman philosophy became interested in Christianity. They studied it, wrote about it and began to adapt the idea of God in Christianity to the Greco-Roman ideal. Many died as martyrs during the early centuries of Christianity.

Finally, in 312 A.D. the emperor Constantine became a Christian and legalized Christianity. During those early centuries a great divide had developed between the church in the West, struggling in Western Europe and North Africa, and the church in the East, moving along the lines the Greco-Roman world could understand. Now, that Christianity was accepted as the empire's legal religion, a basic problem arose. What precisely was Christianity's doctrine of God?[27] Was the Father to whom Jesus referred actually God or was Jesus God? How could Jesus be God and yet be a man, too? And if he wasn't a man, how could we live and be like him? Developing the answers to these questions split Christianity into bitterly warring camps.

The battle reached a crucial point because a skilled church leader in Alexandria set his thoughts about God to music. Soon sailors and travelers in Egypt, Syria and Asia Minor were singing popular ditties that proclaimed the Father alone was true God. Now not only educated theologians but also ordinary people were debating the issue of just who God really is. To settle this issue the emperor Constantine summoned a synod to Nicaea in modern Turkey.[28]

The result of that meeting was what is known as the Nicene Creed. It established that the Father is creator of all things, visible and invisible, and Jesus, the only Son of the Father, is of the same substance as the Father. The only mention of the Spirit was the last line, "And we believe in the Holy Spirit."[29]

Actually bishops went right on teaching as they had before, and the battle of words as to who God is went on for years. Eventually, three theologians in Eastern Turkey came up with a solution which satisfied the Eastern Church. They also developed a more comprehensive explanation of the Holy Spirit.[30] The result is what is known in theological circles as the Niceno-Constantinopolitan Creed and which is referred to in contemporary Christianity as the Nicene Creed. It has been traditionally ascribed to the Council of Constantinople in 381 A.D. but is not believed to actually have been drawn up by it.[31]

Whatever the origin of what we call the Nicene Creed, it is probably based on what is now known as the much shorter Apostles' Creed. In spite of its name, this creed is not of apostolic origin. Its title is first found around 390 A.D. and its present form is first quoted in the early eighth century.[32] It is used extensively in Western Christianity, especially in Baptism.

Here is one final note on the Christian creed which is now called the Nicene Creed. Greek and Russian Orthodox Christians found its explanations of the Trinity resulted in an inspiring religious experience for them. Western Christians found the Trinity simply baffling. It was Augustine who lived in the late fourth and early fifth centuries who defined the Trinity for Western Christianity. No other theologian, except for St. Paul, has been more influential in Western Christianity. He was, however, slow to commit to Christianity because he believed it required celibacy. It is said that he used to pray, "Lord, give me chastity, but not yet."[33]

Initial reaction to that prayer brings an understanding chuckle as Augustine acknowledges his humanity and sexuality. The impact of that acknowledgment, however, tainted Christianity right up to current times. Augustine believed that God had condemned humanity to eternal damnation simply because of Adam's one sin, and the inherited guilt was passed on to all his descendants through the sexual act. "What is the difference," he wrote to a friend," whether it is in a wife or a mother, it is still Eve the temptress that we must beware of in any woman.[34]

On a positive note, Augustine can truly be called the founder of the Western Spirit. In his writings he concluded that one could not search for God in the external world. He believed that God was not an objective reality but rather a spiritual presence in the complex depths of the self. He shared this idea not only with Greek philosophers but also with Hindus and Buddhists as well.[35] As for those of us who are Christians, we need not rely only on Augustine to learn that God is within us. We can go straight to Jesus who tells us, "And I will pray the Father and he will give you another Counselor…even the Spirit of truth…you know him, for he dwells with you, and will be in you."[36]

Never having been a fan of Augustine because of his anti-feminism, I felt properly chastised when I realized it was he who stressed God's Spirit within us. Now, more than fifteen centuries later, I find the science of Quantum Physics can indicate our Spirit within us may be invisible but is nevertheless real. It can actually consist of myriads of subatomic entities dancing rapidly, creating themselves anew as well as new entities and giving off life-enhancing energy.

While Augustine's concept of our God's Spirit remained not only constant but also strengthened in the beliefs of the church, Christianity's history of dancing has been sporadic. In the first five centuries of Christianity dance was acceptable because it was part of the Judaic tradition.[37] In fact, in the two earliest Christian liturgies recorded in detail, dance is used in the order of service.[38]

By the fourth and fifth centuries, however, many references to dancing in worship appear to warn against any activity that hinted of Roman degeneracy. Almost foretelling what science would suggest centuries later, emphasis moved away from the physical movement in dancing to it being symbolic of the spiritual motions of the soul.[39]

In the Middle Ages different dance traditions emerged. One, in particular, centered around dance performed by the clergy as part of the Mass.[40] Another performed by worshipers for special ceremonies or festivals took the form of processions though ring or round dances were popular also. Actually, the dances were performed to hymns or carols, the word "carol" being derived from the Latin *corolla* meaning ring while "caroler" comes from the Latin *choraula* which means "flute-player for chorus-dancing."[41]

Over the centuries the popularity of religious dancing continued, peaked into actual mania at such times as during the period of the Black Plague from 1347 to 1373, then waning during the turbulent years during and following the Reformation. While the leaders of the Protestant Reformation were critical of traditional church customs and tended to view dancing from an erotic perspective, Martin Luther was not against dance. He actually wrote a carol for children in which two stanzas support the role of song and dance in worship. In the years after the Reformation both Protestant and Catholic churches chose to exclude dancing as part of religious liturgy.[42]

Happily, however, during the twentieth century there has been considerable liturgical renewal and dance has become not only acceptable but featured as a special expression of Christian worship. I remember particularly a beautiful group of modern ballet dancers at a Christmas Eve Service in the Chapel at Princeton University in the late 1980's.

Against this background, one wonders whether or not Jesus of Nazareth himself danced. Since he was a devout Jew and dancing was part of his religious heritage, it's reasonable to assume that he did. One can almost visualize him joining in a joyous dancing of the Hora at the Wedding of Cana, all rejoicing that the best wine was served at last.

Which thought takes us back to the hymn with which this review of Christianity began, Sydney Carter's *Lord of the Dance*. Remember the description of Jesus, "He dances that shape and pattern which is at the heart of our reality." If we are moved to that conviction, then Jesus is truly a first century prophet suggesting the scientific reality that we are all a "Dancing Spirit?"

As I read over the next three verses of the hymn, Jesus becomes real for me in a totally contemporary way. He is human, a man with a mission, filled with love for his suffering people, gifted to help them, but caught in a web of politics and power. In the depths of his being is his eternal Spirit, God within him, inspiring and urging him on to fulfill his destiny. Every positive emotion of reaching out encourages those myriads of invisible but very real subatomic entities within him to dance faster and faster. Think of him like that as you read:

> I danced for the scribe and the pharisee,
> But they would not dance and they wouldn't follow me.
> I danced for the fishermen, for James and John;
> They came with me and the dance went on
>
> I danced on the Sabbath and I cured the lame;
> The holy people said it was a shame.
> They whipped and they stripped and they hung me on high,
> And they left me there on the cross to die.
>
> I danced on a Friday when the sky turned black.
> It's hard to dance with the devil on your back.
> They buried my body and they thought I'd gone,
> But I am the Dance, and I still go on.[43]

From the Apostle Paul and the writers of the Gospels...to the early theologians like Augustine who fashioned the tenets of traditional Christianity...to the reformers from the fifteenth and sixteenth centuries on like Martin Luther and John Calvin...to the many variations of Christianity which exist today...are we moving into a New Age of Spirituality? As Physics has moved from the Newtonian perspective to Quantum Physics, is Christianity moving from a limited view of humanity's relationship with God? Is it possible that as each blind man sees the elephant differently, we may be spiritually blind? Does science now point the way to how each of us, no matter how we view God, can help our Spirit to dance, as Jesus did, through love of all?

> They cut me down and I leapt up high,
> I am the life that'll never, never die;
> I'll live in you if you'll live in me;
> I am the Lord of the Dance, said he.
>
> Dance, then, wherever you may be,
> I am the Lord of the Dance, said he;
> And I'll lead you all, wherever you may be,
> And I'll lead you all in the Dance, said he.[4]

I am a Christian, born and bred into the milieu of a Christian family life from birth through childhood, puberty and as a young adult. As such, I respond almost innately with positive emotions to the words of *Lord of the Dance*. For me, Jesus of Nazareth is the paradigm for how to live and die. As he led in the dance of his life, so would I follow, convinced that his is the way, and the only way, to find hope and joy both here and hereafter.

I am, however, a human being, well-traveled around the world and reasonably well-read in the history and literature of other religions. Through Rotary International, an apolitical and non-religious service organization in 166 countries with 1.2 million members, in which my husband has been active for more than fifty years, we have made friends worldwide. Whether it is our Indian Hindu friends from New Delhi, our Japanese friends from Tokyo, our Muslim friends in the United States and abroad, or many friends from Europe and Asia who are not religious, if they are active in Rotary International, they are committed to reach out to others. More than any single religious group in my experience, Rotarians exemplify the "Dancing Spirit" which can contribute to hope and joy not just for one's self but for all humanity. A Rotarian never asks what the religious faith is of one for whom the check is written or the helping hand extended.

Such background and associations have broadened my perspective as a Christian and, as a committed Christian, I feel compelled to share with others. It is my belief that Quantum Physics illustrates the paradigm for Christianity. It shows from a scientific perspective that we are created to live in unity with others, literally bumping into, touching, helping and healing others. As we do so we literally recreate ourselves as we create new life for others, giving off life-enhancing energy to all around us. That is what Jesus, God's Christ, did and that is true Christianity.

◆   ◆   ◆

Do not argue with the followers of earlier revelation
otherwise than in the most kindly manner—unless it be
such of them as are set on evil doing—and say: "We believe
in that which has been bestowed upon us, as well as that
which has been bestowed upon you: for our God and your
God is one and the same, and it is unto him that we (all)
surrender ourselves."

—The Koran 29:46

Islam shares its basic belief in the One God with both Judaism and Christianity. The word Islam is Arabic for surrender, and a Muslim is one who surrenders to God. Unlike Christianity, however, Muslims do not insist that theirs is the only way to relate to the One God, as is evidenced from the quotation above from the Koran.

The Koran is Islam's Holy Scripture, as the Hebrew Bible is to Judaism and the entire Bible, including the New Testament, is to Christians. It teaches that God has sent messengers to every people on earth.[45] Such a Muslim belief reflects the paradigm for all humanity which appears to be revealed in the latest Quantum Physics research. Like the tiny subatomic entities interact with each other, Muslims wish to relate to, literally bump into and fully coexist with others in a multi-religious world.

Like all faiths, Islam arose out of the needs of a people to understand who they were, what was the meaning of life, how did it begin and where did it lead. As with Buddhism and its Buddha and Christianity with Jesus, there was a special individual, a prophet blessed with special insight, who founded Islam.

It all began about 610 A.D. in Arabia. Muhammad ibn Abdallah, a member of the Quraysh tribe, took his family to Mount Hira just outside Mecca for a special religious retreat during the month of Ramadan. This was a common custom amongst Arabs, and Muhammad would spend time praying to the Arab High God and giving out food and alms to the poor.[46]

A thoughtful and sensitive man, Muhammad was apparently concerned about his people. Only a few generations earlier they had lived a harsh nomadic life in the area, but in recent years positive changes occurred. Mecca had become the most active and important trading center in the area and Muhammad and his people had become rich beyond their wildest dreams. In the old days, each member of the tribe knew he or she was dependent on all others for survival. Banded together, they took care of the poor and vulnerable members, recognizing the value of all. It was different now. Individuals were beginning to build personal fortunes and the community ideal was sacrificed to individualism. Muhammad feared that unless his tribe would put more true value in the place of their greed and egotism, the tribe would break apart morally and politically.[47]

As is obvious from the description of his family's annual pilgrimage, the Bedouin tribes of the area had a religion of sorts. They even had a shrine, the Kabah, a massive cube-shaped building in Mecca. It was very old and believed to have been originally dedicated to al-Lah, the High God of the Arabs.

Nor were the Arab tribes living around Mecca isolated from other religious faiths. There were some Jewish and Christian communities in the area.[48] Mecca was also a trading center. Merchants who traveled to Syria and Iraq brought back stories and the Arabs were also surrounded by Persia (Iran) and the Byzantine empire.[49] Some of the Christians and Jews with whom they came in contact occasionally taunted them for having no revelation from God and no Holy Scriptures. This gave the Arabs a feeling of inferiority.[50]

With all these outside influences, Muhammad had come to believe that the High God of the Arabs was the same God worshiped by Jews and Christians. He also thought this God would have to send a prophet to the Arabs, just like Jesus was sent to the Christians and Moses to the Jewish people, but he never thought he would be that prophet.[51]

Then, on that fateful trip in the early seventh century, Muhammad spent a night on Mt. Hira. There he believed an angel from al-Lah, the Arab High God, appeared to him in a dream. When he awoke, he believed he saw al-Lah. As a result of this experience, he believed he had been called by the One God to be a prophet to his people. He began almost immediately to recite messages in Arabic which he believed were spoken to him by the Angel Gabriel. Over time, through these messages, he challenged his people to practice love towards the poor, the slaves and foreigners. He also spoke of the resurrection of the dead[52] and the Last Day, when God would judge humans and assign them to heaven or hell.[53]

It was said Muhammad would go into a trance, even lose consciousness and lower his head between his knees. This was a position adopted by contemporary Jewish mystics when they entered an alternative state of consciousness but Muhammad had no way of knowing this.[54]

Since Muhammad could neither read nor write, as each new message from the Angel Gabriel was spoken aloud by Muhammad, the Muslims would learn it by heart. Those few who were literate would write down what they heard Muhammad recite. It wasn't until some twenty years after Muhammad's death that the first official copy was made of the *qur'an* (the recitation) or what we now know as the Koran.[55]

The various suras or chapters of the Koran can be dated with reasonable accuracy. It is not a narrative like parts of the Hebrew Bible or the Christian New Testament. Instead it deals with various themes like God's presence in the world, the life of the prophets or the Last Judgment. Nor is it meant to be read as Christians read their Bible but rather recited aloud.[56] It even speaks of an afterlife, as these words indicate:

> ...in the end he (God) causes him to die and brings him to the grave; and then, if it be his will, he shall raise him again to life.[57]

Unlike Christianity, however, Islam has no obligatory doctrines which must be accepted. They believe in the One God rather than the Christian concept of God as a Trinity. Nor do they believe in the Incarnation which is that Jesus is both human and divine, God come to earth in the human person of a Son of God. They call these *zanna* which is Arabic for guesswork, a term used in the Koran for pointless theological speculation or self-indulgent guesswork.[58]

The Koran also stresses the need for intelligence in seeing the work and messages of God in the world. Muslims are not to turn from reason but to look at life with curiosity. This enabled them to build a fine tradition of natural science, often seen as a danger by Christianity. For example, the stories of the prophets, the accounts of the Last Judgment, and even the joys of paradise are not to be interpreted literally but rather as myths of a higher, still unknown reality.

As eagerly as his people in the vicinity of Mecca originally accepted Muhammad's messages from the one High God, many rejected the idea that they could no longer worship the traditional gods as they always had. Like Jesus of Nazareth, the establishment turned against him and he and about seventy other Muslims and their families moved to Medina in 622. This marks the beginning of the Islamic calendar and, from this time on, Muhammad was more fortunate than Jesus. Islam became a political power as well as a religion, with Muhammad as its head.[59] Frequent prayers, almsgiving and fasting were advocated as was a pilgrimage to Mecca, just as Jews in Jesus' time made their pilgrimage to Jerusalem.

All did not go smoothly in Medina, however. There were three large Jewish tribes in the area and at first they were friendly and welcomed the Muslims. As they saw their prominence in the area being threatened by the newcomers, however, the Jews became antagonistic and often laughed at and taunted the Islam followers. This was a deep disappointment to Muhammad, but he did learn much of value from the Jewish people and struggled to adapt his religion to bring it closer to Judaism as he understood it. One very special story from the Jewish Scriptures provided a new meaning and authenticity for Islam. It is the story of another son of Abraham, one born before Isaac who was the son of Sarah, Abraham's wife.

In the Hebrew Scriptures, Abraham also had had a son by his concubine Hagar. Later, when his wife Sarah gave birth to Isaac, she became jealous and demanded that Abraham get rid of Hagar and her son Ishmael. To comfort Abraham, God promised that Ishmael would also be the father of a great nation. To this story the Arabian Jews had made some additions of their own. Local legend was that Abraham had left Hagar and Ishmael in the valley of Mecca. Later he visited them and together father and son built the Kabah, the first temple of the One God. Thus Ishmael became father of the Arabs and so, like the Jews, Arabs also were sons of Abraham.[60]

In January of 624 the new religion of al-Lah declared its independence and Muhammad commanded that Muslims pray facing Mecca instead of Jerusalem. This changing the direction of prayer has been considered Muhammad's most creative religious gesture.[61] While total acceptance by all Arabs did not come easily, in 630 the city of Mecca opened its gates to Muhammad. In 632, shortly before his death, he made what has been called the Farewell Pilgrimage to Mecca. It was then that he Islamized the old Arabian pagan rites of the *hajj* or pilgrimage as a duty to be carried out by all Muslims at least once in their life, circumstances permitting. He then died unexpectedly after a short illness in June 632.[62]

All did not go smoothly after Muhammad's death. There was an immediate struggle over leadership. A close friend of Muhammad was selected by a majority to take over Islam but many felt that Muhammad's son-in-law should have been the successor. Ultimately this resulted in a split, with Muhammad's son-in-law heading the Shiah-i-Ali as a minority which defied the majority Sunnah. In 680 in a battle between the two factions, Muhammad's grandson was killed. He thus became a martyr and remains a hero for the Shiah.[63]

By this time the Muslims began to establish their empire, which eventually included not only Arabs in the surrounding Byzantine and Persian empires but continued into Asia and North Africa. Nowhere in the empire were people forced to become Muslims. At some times and in some places it was actually forbidden by law. Muslims believed that they were committed to implementing a just society. Their political health was as important to them as theological principles were to Christians.

During the ninth century Arabs came into contact with Greek science and philosophy. They studied astronomy, alchemy, medicine and mathematics and, by the tenth century, had achieved more scientific discoveries than in any other previous period of history. A new type of Muslim emerged, referred to as Falsafahs. They wanted to live rationally in accordance with the laws that they believed governed the cosmos, which could be discerned at every level of reality. It was important for them to find a link between their faith and a more rational outlook.[64]

Even more interesting than the rational Falsafahs, however, are the mystics of Islam. And there are many, from those who experience the once-in-a-lifetime *hajj* to Mecca to the Whirling Dervish Sufis from Konya in modern Turkey. They remind one of Jesus of Nazareth who promised us the Spirit within or Augustine who wrote of the mystical experience which he and his Mother shared and how he described it: "Our minds were lifted up by an ardent affection towards eternal being itself."[65]

As for Muslims, many who are not even Arabs make the pilgrimage to Mecca to circumambulate the Kabah, shrine of the One God. Putting their everyday anxieties and selfish motives aside, they gather together as a community. As they begin their walk, they cry out: "Here I am at your service O al-Lah." Then walk around, closer and closer to the shrine of al-Lah. The emotion aroused is described by the late Iranian philosopher Ali Shariati:

> As you circumambulate and move closer to the Kabah, you feel like a small
> stream merging with a big river. Carried by a wave you lose touch with the

ground. Suddenly, you are floating, carried on by the flood. As you approach the centre, the pressure of the crowd squeezes you so hard that you are given a new life. You are now part of the People, you are now a Man, alive and eternal...The Kabah is the world's sun whose face attracts you into its orbit. You have become part of this universal system. Circumambulating around Al-lah, you will soon forget yourself...You have been transformed into a particle that is gradually melting and disappearing. This is absolute love at its peak.[66]

This description reminds one not only of the desired results of meditation or prayer but, even moreso, of those tiny subatomic entities now revealed in Quantum Physics who whirl their way to create and recreate. The *hajj* offers each Muslim the mystical experience of moving inward toward the center to reach al-Lah, the One God. Once they enter the hallowed sanctuary of Kabah, all violence is forbidden. No one may speak a harsh word.

While many Muslims may know the mystical experience of the *hajj* only once in a lifetime, one group developed their own mystical traditions. They are known as the Sufis and they formed during the eighth and ninth centuries. Wanting to return to a simple life in an evermore complicated world, they dressed in coarse white garments made of wool (SWF) that were supposed to have been favored by Muhammad. Thus they were known as Sufis. They particularly believed in the unity of all religions and, as a result, Jesus was highly regarded by them They were even known to say, "There is no god but al-Lah and Jesus is his messenger."[67]

The most famous of the Sufis are the Mawlawiyyah or the Mevlevi Order, whose members are known in the West as the Whirling Dervishes. Their founder is Jalal ad-Din Rumi, also known as Jalaluddin or Celaleddin Rumi. His followers called him Mawlana or Mevlana which means guide or master. He was born in 1207 in what is today Afghanistan but moved with his family to Konya in modern Turkey, which was then the Seljak Empire.

Rumi's father, a noted Islamic preacher determined to have his son well-educated, accomplished that goal by the time Rumi was thirty-three years old. Four years later Rumi met a spiritual vagabond known as Shams who had a profound impact on his life. An eminent professor of religion, Rumi then became an inspired poet and a great lover of humanity.

With the help of a friend who served as his scribe, Rumi wrote the great poetic *Masnawi,* which became known as the Sufi Bible. In it Rumi challenged his followers to find the transcendent dimension in human life and to see through physical reality to the hidden reality within. Quantum Physics now illustrates that invisible reality of all physical life. Just so, the work of such prophets as Rumi and the many religions of our world tell us of the invisible reality of our own Spirit and the One God whose Spirit empowers and is the source for our inner Spirit.

To come to the realization of our Spirit within and make contact with God who empowers us is what inspires the Sufis to dance. Their dance is one of the most exquisite of spiritual rituals. In it the dancers, or Semazens as they are called, whirl rapidly about sixty times per minute, in order to achieve a state of trance. The haunting music of the reed flute which accompanies them symbolizes the Divine Breath which gives life to everything. Through their whirling the dancers relinquish their earthly life to be reborn in mystical union with God. As they dance they raise their right hand palm-up to receive the blessings of heaven, with their left hand palm-down to transfer those blessings to earth.[68] This passage from the *Masnawi* describes it:

> Listen to the reed, how it tells a tale, complaining of separateness. Ever since I was parted from the reed-bed, my lament has caused men and women to moan…everyone who is left far from his source wishes back the time when he was united to it.[69]

Along with major religions of the East and the earlier religions of Judaism and Christianity in the West, Islam also reflects that invisible reality which Quantum Mechanics reveals.

◆   ◆   ◆

Fact and Faith Come Together: When we compared the four basic conclusions reached in a review of Quantum Physics research with the three major Eastern religions, we found that the similarities were striking. The same is true with the three major Western religions, especially Christianity. As the subatomic entities of life engage in their invisible dance in scientific research, so Western religions present the same basic paradigms for life, namely:

1. The unity of the universe.

2. Matter converts to energy and energy cannot be destroyed.

3. Choices made impact results achieved.

4. The truth is found deep within.

1. The unity of the universe: No single subatomic entity lives in isolation but only in a dancing relationship with others, even non-locally or faster than the speed of light.

> **Judaism**, more than any of the Eastern religions, exhibits humanity bound together in common commitment that is unique. Individuals of Jewish heritage can probably be best understood from a vibrant and active group context, just like the dancing relationships of subatomic entities in Quantum Physics.
> **Christianity** has at its core the teachings and life of Jesus who lived as though humanity was bound together in unity. Jew or Samaritan, pillar of society or prostitute, male or female, he touched them all through his healing touch or loving act.
> **Islam** illustrates its belief in the unity of the universe in the *hajj*. It has been described like this. "You have become part of the universal system…transformed into a particle…" It sounds like a forecast of Quantum Physics research.

2. Matter converts to energy and energy cannot be destroyed: Subatomic particles change form in their dancing relationship with each other, sacrificing themselves, then resurrecting as they give off energy as light, an energy which cannot be destroyed.

> **Judaism**, through pogroms and holocaust, has prevailed as its members exhibited self-sacrifice and tenacious love for the life of the entire people. So Quantum Physics sets the pattern for sacrifice leading to new life which cannot be destroyed.
> **Christianity** as lived by Jesus is the paramount example of sacrificial love. In Quantum Physics the subatomic entities self-sacrifice because it is their nature. Jesus made the choice, which reminds us of his resurrection and our theme song, "I am the life that'll never, never die; I'll live in you…"
> **Islam** illustrates its dedication to self-sacrificial living in the *hajj*, so aptly-described like this: "…the crowd squeezes you so hard that you are given a new life." This, too, sounds like a forecast of the paradigm set by Quantum Physics research.

3. Choices made impact results achieved: Choices made by the tester in Quantum Physics determine how waves or particles will be studied and, thus, the results that may be achieved. Just so we use our abilities and characteristics to make choices which help to form the person we become.

Judaism has continued the struggle for new life generation after generation by following the teachings of the Torah. As a result its members have made outstanding contributions to society wherever they live, confirming that choices made impact results just as they do in Quantum Physics research.

Christianity, when viewed from the life of Jesus, has inspired generation after generation to live in love for others. Jesus taught that choices made determine joy and hope in this life and for the life hereafter and Quantum Physics now verifies that truth.

Islam was established by Muhammad so his people would not succumb to greed and egotism. The Koran, a guide to living, can help each one avoid being apart from but rather a part of all of life, just as Quantum Physics verifies choices made impact results.

4. The truth is found deep within: Quantum Physics discovered the basic dancing entities of life by research at greater depths than ever thought possible. Just so humans meditate and pray, reaching deep within for the truth, the encouragement and the reassurance that each of us is truly a Dancing Spirit living in relationship with all others.

Judaism encourages prayer and study as well as meditation. Like Eastern religions, Judaism uses prayer for a deeper understanding of spirituality, individually and in public worship. They also find positive inspiration and encouragement in dance or music. For proof one need only join in dancing or even watching as others dance the Hora at a Jewish wedding or listen to the music of many of the renowned Jewish composers.

Christianity encourages prayer and meditation or centering prayer and Jesus set an example both in his life and death. Christians are assured that the Spirit is always available to help us dance through life to the rhythm set by our "Lord of the Dance." Jesus leads us as we follow him in the dance of a loving life which leads us to the heaven of a life of loving.

Islam encourages reaching deep within for spiritual contact through an almost hypnotic reading of the Koran, in rituals like the *hajj* or in the dance of the Whirling Dervish. All are analogous to the reaching deeply within us to touch the reality of our Dancing Spirit, whose existence Quantum Physics research now reveals.

5

East Joins West in a "New Age" Dance

To turn, to turn 'twill be our delight
'Til by turning, turning, we come round right.

—*Simple Gifts[1]*

The last two lines of the old Shaker tune *Simple Gifts* quoted above sum up a simple message: We dance through life, turning and turning, 'til we come out right...'til we learn to share in love and delight. That is a paraphrase of the message which is found in this simple song with a profound message. And that in essence is what the "New Age" Dance is all about.

Of course, it isn't called a dance. Some refer to it or think of it as a religion. According to Webster's Dictionary, religion is "the service and worship of God or the supernatural." The New Age movement can be both more or less than that. In fact, it isn't new either but actually has evolved out of truth and practices older than recorded history. Before we start tracing its roots though, let's clarify exactly what we mean by the New Age movement or New Age Spirituality.

It grew out of the restlessness, frustration and needs of the younger generation in the late 1960s. They were plagued by the demands of the Vietnam War, the political and social turbulence it created, and the seeming failure of traditional religions to calm, sustain and inspire them. Like generations before them in this country and all around our globe, they wanted meaning and purpose in life, and they reached out for what was offered to them. It was the New Age, the Age of Aquarius, and in that New Age the young searchers found the spiritual and ethical guidance they craved.

Each astrological age is said to last 2000 years. The previous Age of Pisces with the fish as its symbol, and known to us as the Christian era, began with the birth of Jesus. It drew to a close as we were about to enter the third millennium. The energy believed to have entered the earth plane during the Pisces Age was agape or love of one human being for another, because we are all members of the family of humanity.

For Christians especially it is Jesus, God's Christ, which word in Greek really means "anointed one," who brought that energy into our world. His most remarkable lesson taught in his words to humanity was, "Love one another as I have loved you."[2] And he not only spoke that message but lived out the full essence of what it meant when he died in love for others.

With the advent of the Age of Aquarius, a new age was born and with it a new message, an evolution in human thinking. That message is that not only are we individual members of the same family but, together as a whole entity, we are responsible for all humanity and for the earth on which we live. It's interesting to note here that just as the Age of Aquarius ushers in the oneness of humanity and the totality of our responsibility for all on earth, so Quantum Physics is uncovering the oneness and unity of the entire cosmos. And it does so by showing us, through the actions of subatomic entities which are the building blocks of all visible and invisible life, that self-sacrifice not only recreates ourselves but produces new productive life as well. This sounds more like a new affirmation of an age-old message rather than just an interesting coincidence.

Where did this young generation find their message, or rather messages, for New Age Spirituality has many facets? A backward look gives us a clue. Remember how the ancient Sumarians absorbed beliefs and gods from the Akkadians just north of them? Remember how Abraham borrowed from them and then how his descendant, Moses, borrowed from the Egyptians amongst whom he was raised? Remember how the Israelites merged ideas from the religions of the Canaanites into what came to be Judaism? Remember how Christianity borrowed from Judaism and from the influences not only of Greek culture but of some of the cults which existed in their part of the world as Christianity was evolving in the first centuries after Jesus' life and death? Remember how Islam evolved from many of the beliefs of Judaism and Christianity as well as the remnants of religious beliefs of the ancient Arabs?

New Age Spirituality was no different. It evolved out of what was readily available. The one big difference is that, by the twentieth century, worldwide communication had shrunk our world and there was much from which to choose. Immigrants from the Far East with their many different beliefs had settled in America's Far West, especially California. Stories of the spiritual beliefs of Native Americans were part of our heritage. More young people were becoming college-educated and learning about other cultures. More people were traveling and personally experiencing other cultures. And, so very important, science was taking giant strides. From medicine to psychology to chemistry and physics, new insights opened to both the physical and spiritual aspects of life.

The New Age generation borrowed from them all but still maintained its uniqueness. Unlike established religions, New Age Spirituality has no Holy Scriptures, no central governing body, no enlisted membership, no ordained clergy, no creed or dogma. It is a free, open, searching movement dedicated to enriching the spiritual dimension of all who participate in it. Even more important, it does not demand that its way is the only way to spiritual hope and joy nor does it insist that you forsake all other beliefs about the spiritual dimension of life.

Where, how and to what New Age Spirituality looked for its beginnings is probably buried in the mists and mysteries of primitive societies. Even those early clans and tribes had their shamans and medicine men, individuals who were blessed with special knowledge and powers. Those gifts have been passed on through the generations to specially gifted individuals in our time as well. Any doubters of that phenomenon need only read recorded religious history.

Whether one searches in the annals of Buddhism in the Far East or Judaism in the Western World, there is record after record of spiritually gifted individuals. Of course, particularly in the religions of the Western World, especially Western as opposed to Eastern Christianity, emphasis has been on the intellectual aspects of religion. We learned that when we reviewed the many theological debates, negotiations and special synods or meetings of the first centuries of Christianity, which eventually resulted in the doctrines of the Trinity and the Nicene and Apostles Creeds.

That having been said, however, even the intellectuals in Western Christianity had their spiritual insights. As a prime example we cite St. Augustine's record of a spiritual encounter with God, an experience he shared with his mother as a participant. He described it as an ascent to heaven or God which, from a spiritual perspective, is considered the furthest reach of the human spirit. Augustine told of the event not as a literal journey but as a mental ascent to a reality within. He described it like this:

> Our minds were lifted up by an ardent affection towards eternal being itself. Step by step we climbed beyond all corporate objects and the heaven itself, where sun, moon and stars shed light on the earth. We ascended even further by internal reflection and dialogue and wonder at your works and entered into our own minds.[3]

It's interesting to note that this description of an "ascent" is not unusual. People all over the world and at all times in history have given witness of this kind of contemplative experience. Those who believe in the One God tend to describe it as a "vision of God." Buddhists have called it a glimpse of "Nirvana." It has become obvious throughout history that some humans, no matter what their religion or belief, have the ability to achieve that subjective experience of penetrating inward to meet with the original source and ultimate goal. Augustine told of it in even more detail when he elaborated on the experience he and his mother shared.

> Therefore we said: If to anyone the tumult of the flesh has fallen silent, if the images of earth, water, and air are quiescent, if the heavens themselves are shut out and the very soul itself is making no sound and is surpassing itself by no longer thinking about itself, if all dreams and visions in the imagination are excluded, if all language and everything transitory is silent—for if anyone could hear then this is what all of them would be saying, "We did not make ourselves, we were made by him who abides for eternity" (Psalm 79:3, 5)... That is how it was when at that moment we extended our reach and in a flash of mental energy attained the eternal wisdom which abides beyond all things.[4]

Augustine did not feel either that he and his mother were exclusive in their ability to penetrate inward to "the eternal wisdom which abides beyond all things." He believed other privileged persons were sometimes able to see God and cited particularly Moses and St. Paul.[5]

Throughout the centuries, from Far East to Far West, across all boundaries of religions and belief systems, contemplative individuals have and, more now than ever before, do strive to go beyond all thoughts, all images, all mind and memory to rise above the physical and reach that inner core of being. It is there they hope to find the joy of love and peace, whether they view it as God, as their source and their ultimate goal, or as their true and real eternal Spirit.

No matter if it's Moses, St. Paul, Augustine, the achingly breathtaking dance of the Whirling Dervish, or you or me, the desire to know God or our Spirit within is a basic need and hunger for all humankind. The meditation of the Buddhist Monk, the centering prayer of the Christian, the dance of the Dervish or the simple meditation or centering prayer of someone like you or me, the search for the Spirit of God or our own Spirit center is timeless and universal.

Thanks to the Far East traveling to the Far West, as Asian immigrants made their way to California especially, restless and anxiety-filled young New Agers were captivated by the custom, the act and art of meditation. To pray is to speak to God, we Christians say. But to meditate, to be still and go inward to where

God's Spirit may touch our inner Spirit, is the way to listen to God. That is why, whatever their background, most followers of New Age Spirituality believe in and practice the act and art of meditation. It fulfills the promise of *Simple Gifts*. It helps them turn round and round in life, 'til they come out right. It inspires and encourages them to share in love and delight, to join in the dance of life which brings hope and joy here and hereafter.

Of course, one can't help wonder about precisely what it is New Agers are looking for or listening to. Do they believe in God, in Jesus, in Mohammad or Buddha? How do they learn about loving and sharing? They have no Holy Scripture, no specific church, no guides or rules, no minister or priest. What do they believe and how and why? Actually, they have not only absorbed the act and art of meditation from the Far East. They have learned about karma and reincarnation in the process also.

Karma simply means that the good and bad deeds we do in life determine how we will be rewarded or punished in our next life, for those who believe in reincarnation. Reincarnation, of course, means that when we leave this earth we go to the spiritual plane or dimension until we are born again into the life which our karma has determined.

Whether you call it karma, good and evil, right and wrong, or selflessness and sin, it means somewhat the same in any philosophy or religion. The motivations for choosing to engage in one or the other and the scope of one's choice are what are different. Christians choose how to live, whether in selflessness or sin, guided by the life and lessons of Jesus. We try to live in love for one another as Jesus taught, "Love one another as I have loved you." (John 5:12). New Agers, as part of their borrowing from Eastern religions, believe in the connectedness of all of life and, therefore, accept the premise of responsibility for all humanity and for all the earth. That's why so many New Agers are involved in groups concerned with the shrinking resources of our globe, endangered species, and minorities of color, creed, sexual orientation and socio-economic deprivation. All are our responsibility, according to many New Agers. How we meet these responsibilities determines our karma. For many New Agers, our karma may apply to a future lifetime as well as determine how hopeful, how joyful, how fulfilled we are in this lifetime.

Reincarnation is more complicated because by its very meaning it implies a belief in a spiritual reality or dimension and successive lifetimes. It is my experience from my visitations as a minister to those who are ill, aged and/or unable to move around freely, almost everyone responds to the idea of a spiritual dimension after life on earth. Whether one calls it Paradise, Heaven, Happy Hunting

Ground, Nirvana, going to be with God or whatever doesn't matter. What matters is that it's an end to pain, to anxiety, to fear, and an opportunity to once again meet with loved ones who have gone before us. It's a new beginning.

My impression is that some New Agers accept reincarnation, others may not. For those who do accept it, there is ample evidence for doing so, especially from the advances in the fields of psychology and psychiatry. And don't forget the action of those subatomic entities as they self-sacrifice in their dance of life, then resurrect as well as emit life-enhancing energy for others. Quantum Physics reveals in the dance of the basic units of life the promise of reincarnation.

Frankly, I never actually accepted reincarnation even though I thought it was a really neat idea. The thought of heaven as it is suggested in conservative Christianity always seemed monotonous and boring to me. Life, with its challenges, its opportunities for learning and growing, has its peaks and valleys. That's part of the positive picture, for each peak seems to provide a wider and better view of life, a panorama of possibilities. I must have been fertile ground for a new book that came to my attention.

As a "thank you" for listening while she talked out some personal problems, an acquaintance sent me a copy of *Many Lives, Many Masters*, a book that was written by Dr. Brian Weiss, a psychotherapist who was Chairman of Psychiatry at the Mount Sinai Medical Center in Miami. Dr. Weiss had an impeccable reputation in his profession and distrusted any type of therapy that could not be proved by traditional scientific methods. Then he was challenged by a patient for whom the tried and true methods of treatment simply did not help. After eighteen months with no positive results he decided to try hypnosis.

That decision ultimately ended in a cure for his patient and changed his life and, like mine, probably that of many others, both patients and readers, as well. During the trance states of her treatment, Dr. Weiss's patient recalled "past life" memories that proved to be the cause of many of her emotional problems. Equally as remarkable, she was able to act as a conduit or channel through which was passed information from evolved "spirit entities" about the secrets of life and death. Dr. Weiss had no scientific explanation for what happened but, fortunately, each session had been taped. For several years he hesitated to share this material but finally felt compelled to do so. *Many Lives, Many Masters* was the result.[6] Reading that book set me on a course of research. Many months later, after hours and hours of reading and research, as well as help from my much-better-informed daughter, I became a believer.

Simultaneously, I was interested in researching the probability of prayer consisting of thought waves just as light and sound travel in wave form. That led to the study of Quantum Physics and the latest research with subatomic entities. Combining the two interests, I kept thinking about these subatomic entities, too small to be seen with a microscope. They move so rapidly that they bump into each other, self-sacrifice, emit energy, resurrect and create new entities. If this is the pattern of not only our earth but the entire cosmos, then it must be the pattern for all humanity. We humans live together, bump into each other in our interpersonal relations, hopefully self-sacrifice ourselves for the good of others. In so doing, we emit life-enhancing energy, create new life and resurrect ourselves in the process. It certainly makes sense to me.

The question arises: Do all New Agers believe in reincarnation or progressive lives? Some meditate or practice centering prayer within the context of the religion in which they were raised or in which they are currently participating. Others who may be Christians, whether Catholic or Protestant, may struggle with whether a belief in progressive lives is acceptable or forbidden by their religion. The answers to that are varied.

Going back to antiquity, evidences of belief in rebirth are common. In ancient Judaism, for example, ideas of reincarnation go back to as far as the eighth century B.C.E. In the early days of Christianity reincarnation was also an accepted belief. Josephus, the Jewish historian who lived during most of the first century, records that reincarnation was taught widely at that time.[7]

While it is difficult to point out any clear unambiguous Christian doctrine that tells what happens after death, there are numerous Bible passages which suggest reincarnation. Here is an example:

> *"Who do men say that the Son of man is?" And they said, "Some say John the Baptist, others say Elijah, and others Jeremiah or one of the prophets."*
>
> —Matthew 16:14.

Obviously Jesus was thought of by some to be a prophet from a former lifetime or John the Baptist who had recently been killed and had returned to live again as Jesus. These people must have taken the idea of reincarnation as accepted belief.

Another interesting example from the Christian New Testament involves the story of the miracle which Jesus performed on the man who was born blind. Here is the passage:

As he passed by, he saw a man blind from his birth. And his disciples asked him, "Rabbi, who sinned, this man or his parents?"

—John 9:1.

If the man had been born blind how could his sin have caused the blindness unless that sin had been committed in a previous life? Obviously the disciples who asked the question took reincarnation or previous lives for granted.

There are many additional such references in the Hebrew Bible as well as the Christian New Testament. What happened to these beliefs in the ensuing generations? Actually, they continued in the early Christian communities and with the early Christian Church leaders. It wasn't until the fourth century when Christianity became the official religion of the Roman Empire that the belief in reincarnation began to be a problem. During the next few centuries there was much political and theological unrest between East and West and reincarnation was felt to threaten the stability of the Roman Empire in the West. It appeared to some that perhaps people had to be convinced their salvation must be insured in one lifetime. The idea of past or future lives might weaken the hold of the church over its followers. The result was that the doctrine of reincarnation was declared heretical.

The view in Christianity today has softened somewhat from this viewpoint and depends on which denomination, or even which Pastor, Preacher or Priest, one consults. Most Protestant denominations have no specific ruling and, as with many social and religious problems such as slavery, homosexuality, and others, the Bible can be used to the advantage of either position or proved to substantiate neither.

Roman Catholicism is more complicated. On one hand, the Catechism of the Catholic Church (2116) has this to say:

> All forms of divination are to be rejected: recourse to Satan or demons, conjuring up the dead or other practices falsely supposed to "unveil" the future. Consulting horoscopes, astrology, palm readings, interpretation of omens and lots, the phenomena of clairvoyance, and recourse to mediums all conceal a desire for power over time, history, and, in the last analysis, other human beings, as well as a wish to conciliate hidden powers. They contradict the honor, respect, and loving fear that we owe to God alone.

Perhaps a key word in that passage is the word "falsely" and how that distinction might relate to the obvious legitimate records of a renowned psychotherapist such as Dr. Brian Weiss.

Obviously, just as in any human enterprise, there are those in religion and in the "helping professions" who take advantage of others. Contrarily, there have been legitimate strides in medicine and all areas of science to uncover the previously unknown to the benefit of humanity.

While many in Roman Catholicism frown on the belief in reincarnation, many highly educated and dedicated individuals in positions of authority have researched the subject and do not condemn the belief. Interesting, too, is the fact that several of the most noted individuals in the United States today who are known for their psychic abilities come from a Roman Catholic background and still reflect or even participate in Catholic worship.

Obviously, the concept of reincarnation as accepted by many New Agers may present a problem for some individuals from conservative religious backgrounds in major Western World religions. For me, Dr. Weiss's work and the research I did following my reading his reports convinced me, as did the experiences and research which I share with you next.

After I had thoroughly researched Dr. Weiss's work and read about additional cases of authentic hypnosis leading to information on progressive lives, another intriguing subject emerged. At a social function one evening, I was sharing stories about my research on reincarnation when a friend spoke up, "Have you read Sylvia Browne?" "Who is she?" I asked. And a new chapter, a new challenge began for me.

Remember my referring to Dr. Weiss's patient who, while under hypnosis, served as a conduit or channel with "evolved spirits" from the spiritual plane? Sylvia Browne does this by going into a self-induced trance and acting as a medium or channel with the spiritual dimension or plane of life. She is a gifted writer, as well, and a "giving" person, who has often shared her gift for the good of others.

Yes, you may now put on your "Doubting Thomas" expression, if you like. Most people do. I did, but no more. Sylvia Browne's reputation as a psychic and spiritual teacher is sound. She has appeared on television on *Larry King Live* and *The Montel Williams Show*. She has assisted Police Departments in solving crimes. She is a #1 Best Selling *New York Times* author. One of my favorites of her books is *Life on the Other Side*.[8]

Her background is as fascinating as her work. She was raised and educated as a Catholic, even taught in Catholic schools for many years before becoming a nationally recognized psychic. Her ability to become a medium between our physical world and the spiritual dimension or plane is, in New Age language, referred to as channeling.

Learning about Sylvia Browne was a revelation for me but not sufficient. It led to more research and the knowledge that there are now, and have been throughout history, many such channelers. Other contemporary well-known mediums or channelers are George Anderson, Van Praagh and John Edward, all raised in the Catholic Church. Of them, only Edward has remained in and has participated in Catholic worship.

Edward was previously a hospital administrator and may, as a result of association with the health field, be sensitive to the special needs of the sick, dying and bereaved. He believes that his work as a medium is truly a ministry to those with special needs. As one who professes to be a practicing Catholic, he often is criticized by those within the church who consider what he does against the ruling of the church. He has pointed out, however, that many nuns, priests, rabbis and various ministers have checked him out, most with positive results.

My experience for nearly three years serving as a volunteer visitation minister certainly has helped me to understand his rationale. In my visits to patients in hospitals, nursing and rehabilitation facilities as well as those who are home-bound, I have learned firsthand how strong are their needs for encouragement, for hope for a future when there appears to be no future for them in this life. The Christian concept of heaven and being with Jesus is helpful but it's vague and they yearn for something more to bring them solace and hope.

Nor am I immune to those yearnings. When one reaches eighty years of age, as I have done, after an active, challenging and fulfilling life, I'm ready for new energy and a new challenge. The latest research in Quantum Mechanics with its message of unity, self-sacrifice and the promise of new life and new energy are like a lighthouse on an increasingly visible rocky shore for me. It also suggests that a spiritual dimension or plane and reincarnation to another living, learning and loving experience back on this earth are exactly what our everlasting and loving God would offer and what Jesus, God's Christ, was trying to tell us about.

In the final analysis, karma and reincarnation have been presented and authenticated. Whether to accept or reject them is up to each New Ager and to each seeker of true hope and joy. Assuming one does accept them, new horizons appear. What goes on in that spiritual dimension? Who is there, do I have access to them, are my loved ones there? Those individuals with the gift of being able to make the crossing over have varying degrees of success and information to share. If you're a traveler, you know not every trip is perfect. I'm a world traveler which is great. Conversely, I have managed to have severe colds or flu in Rome, Jerusalem, St. Petersburg, Vienna and even for my 60th High School Class Reunion in

Illinois. There are no guarantees that every trip in this life or to the spiritual plane is going to be totally successful.

On the other hand, from the records of many who have received messages from the spiritual dimension through hypnosis, self-induced trances or in other ways, there are successes. There are many records of messages from spiritual masters or advisors, messages from loved ones who have crossed over, and evidences of spiritual guides and guardians for us all. Many New Agers accept this. And many of us, in long-established religions but who are still seekers of truth, are open to what authentic psychological, medical and scientific research has to offer.

On that note, I would like to share with you some thoughts received from spiritual guides as expressed in *Messages from the Masters,*[9] also by Dr. Brian Weiss. In his opening comments Dr. Weiss explains that technology and science, while capable of solving problems, can also be used for bad purposes. Only when used with enlightenment, wisdom and balance can they be truly useful. And, according to the messages received from the "Masters," love is the fulcrum of that balance.

Dr. Weiss's description of what love is and does sounds almost like a contemporary version of St. Paul's much loved, much quoted passages on love from the Bible's New Testament in 1 Corinthians 13.[10] Love, Dr. Weiss says, is the ultimate healer. While physicists now know that everything is energy, it is the energy of love that is the most powerful. When we understand this, we have the secret to inner joy, peace and happiness.[11]

What Dr. Weiss promises is exactly what *Dancing Spirits* can hopefully help you understand and achieve. Those invisible but everlasting subatomic entities hidden in our physical bio-body suits, the real you and the real me, dance rapidly, bumping into each other as they self-sacrifice only to emit new energy, recreate themselves and create anew. They are the basic story, the paradigm for our physical life. As we bump into each other in our interpersonal relations, we sacrifice our ego demands in love for others. The result is that we emit the energy of love. It surrounds us, creates an aura around us, touches all who come in contact with us. And, miracle of miracles, we are not destroyed. Instead only our physical bio-body, worn out and no longer useful, is tossed aside. That eternal Spirit, created of those subatomic entities invisible even to the microscope, is at home in the spiritual dimension. It is not an end. It is a reunion with loved ones who can help us adjust to our new way of life. It is a new beginning.

To what extent New Agers or each of us wishes to pursue the messages of the masters and the promise of spiritual guides to help us on this physical plane is a highly personal matter. Some of us find comfort in the Saints to whom we pray,

to the Angels whom we sense watch over us or to the unexplainable voice or
voices without sound that we hear with our inner ear, as we listen in silent prayer.
Which brings up the question: To whom do New Agers turn when they meditate? How do they think about God?

Throughout the ages many names have been given to God, the Supreme
Source or Spirit from whom we all are born. In the Hebrew Scriptures God is
identified like this:

> *Then Moses said to God, "If I come to the people of Israel and say to them,*
> *'The God of your fathers has sent me to you,' and they ask, me, 'What is his*
> *name?' what shall I say to them?" God said to Moses, "I AM WHO I AM."*
> *And he said, "Say this to the people of Israel, 'I AM has sent me to you.'"*
>
> —Exodus 3:13-14

That passage is perhaps more clear, more wise than we moderns probably give
it credit for being. Does it matter if one believes God has personal characteristics
like us or takes some other form? Does it matter if we think of God as the Trinity
or as Jehovah or as al-Lah? One of my favorite Bible passages doesn't do any of
those. It opens up a new realm of possibilities for understanding God. It describes
God as the energy of love.

> *"God is love, and he who abides in love abides in God, and God abides in*
> *him."*
>
> —1 John 4:16b

As a Christian child, I was taught to think of God as the Trinity of Father,
Son and Spirit. As a mature and very old adult, my conception of God is mixed.
On one hand, I am held captive by my childhood view of God the Father whom,
until about age five, I thought was just a super version of my Daddy. Just like my
Daddy, God loved me even when I was not a good girl and, no matter what
broke or went wrong, God could fix it. When things go wrong at age eighty, I
still am apt to send emergency requests to God to please fix it.

A step up from that position in my mind is that we each are blessed with the
genes of God. Just as I carry the genes of my earthly or physical parents, I carry
the genes of my spiritual parent, the genes of God. In the language of Christianity, you may call that God's Spirit.

What God really is, I have no way of knowing now, but I don't think that
matters. The old Hebrew Scriptures had it right. "I AM WHO I AM!" That's the

final word for me. God isn't what we say God is. God is who God is! We do know God is Spirit and as such invisible to the physical eye but we still can feel and experience what is invisible. Since the New Testament says God is love, that's good enough for me. I experience God as love. When someone loves me, God is visible and warmly present to me and in me.

Now, in view of all this, does it really matter what New Agers think about God? The messages from those masters or spiritual guides are messages of the wisdom and rightness of love. Our karma, the good and bad that we do, determines what happens to us in this life and/or a future life. Meditation or centering prayer helps us to get in touch and keep in touch with God, the Spirit, and the spiritual dimension of reality. It seems to me that New Agers who take the pathway of meditation or centering prayer have found what they need to live a calmer, more anxiety-free and happier life.

As for those of us old-timers whose bio-body suits are beginning to sag, look a bit shabby and ready for discarding, perhaps we can learn from the New Agers. Maybe we can start thinking about what kind of a new bio-body suit we'd like to wear next time around. Maybe we can love a little more, get those invisible sub-atomic dancers inside us moving in a more grace-filled manner and so spread an aura of love around us. Maybe we can enjoy renewed hope and joy and give that gift to others as well.

Maybe the singers of that old Shaker song, *Simple Gifts*, and the Quantum Physicists who have uncovered a new paradigm for physical life can show both New Agers and old-timers how to find hope and joy here and hereafter. Maybe together, as we read the words of that wise old Shaker song, we can learn to turn, to turn, 'til it be our delight, to dance, Spirit, dance, 'til we come out right.

> 'Tis the gift to be simple
> 'Tis the gift to be free
> 'Tis the gift to come down where we ought to be
> And when we are in the place just right
> We'll be in the valley of love and delight.
>
> When true simplicity is gained
> To bow and to bend we will not be ashamed
> To turn, to turn 'twil be our delight
> 'Til by turning, turning, we come round right.[12]

Obviously New Age Spirituality is not an established religion with a specific concept of God or Supreme Source, a Holy Scripture, a central leadership or organized groups which meet regularly in a church of their own, but it is a vital and important movement in our society. It not only has met the needs of the younger generation of the 1960s and 1970s, but it increasingly reaches out to mature generations whose needs are not being filled by the faith of their childhood. Just as the United States as a country has become more diversified in the color, culture and country of origin of its people, so the spiritual needs of the population have diversified as well.

The Age of Pisces has run its course and the Age of Aquarius is in its earliest years. It has, along with Quantum Physics, presented us with a new outlook on the invisible world of subatomic entities and the world of our everlasting Spirit. Their similarities are undeniable!

◆   ◆   ◆

Fact and Faith Come Together: We have compared the four basic conclusions reached in a review of Quantum Physics research with the three major Eastern World religions and the three major Western World religions and found their similarities striking. Now a new millennium has dawned and a seemingly new religion spawned—New Age Spirituality. It's true the New Agers have adopted some of the beliefs and customs of the world's age-old faiths but they have branched out as well, especially assisted by the innovations and improvements in the various sciences. As the subatomic entities of life engage in their invisible dance in Quantum Physics, so New Age Spirituality presents the same basic paradigms for life, namely:

1. The unity of the universe.

2. Matter converts to energy and energy cannot be destroyed.

3. Choices made impact results achieved.

4. The truth is found deep within.

1. The unity of the universe: No single subatomic entity lives in isolation but only in a dancing relationship with others, even non-locally or faster than the speed of light.

New Age Spirituality goes even beyond the religions of both East and West in the belief in the unity of our universe. They stress a new message. Just as no single subatomic entity in Quantum Physics research lives in isolation but only in a dancing relationship with others, so New Agers acknowledge the responsibility of one for all, not only other humans but for all the entire universe.

2. <u>**Matter converts to energy and energy cannot be destroyed:**</u> Subatomic particles change form in their dancing relationship with each other, sacrificing themselves, then resurrecting as they give off energy as light, an energy which cannot be destroyed.

New Age Spirituality followers are especially aware of the importance of energy and the conservation of the various materials, use of which produces the energy which the world needs. As a result they are not only moved to give of themselves for the good of all but they are active in caring for and preserving the valuable elements in our universe which are energy producers. Like Quantum Physics, New Agers illustrate the modern example of Dancing Spirits which turn matter into energy which cannot be destroyed.

3. <u>**Choices made impact results achieved:**</u> Choices made by the tester in Quantum Physics determine how waves or particles will be studied and, thus, the results that may be achieved. Just so we use our abilities and characteristics to make choices which help to form the person we become.

New Age Spirituality followers make choices about how to live not only in relationship with others but with the physical earth on which they live. Many practice yoga or similar physical exercises and follow special diets which include naturally grown food and fresh herbs. In addition they dedicate themselves and their time to preservation of natural resources and care of the environment. Their choices impact results achieved.

4. <u>**The truth is found deep within:**</u> Quantum Physics discovered the basic dancing entities of life by research at greater depths than ever thought possible. Just so humans meditate and pray, reaching deep within for the truth, the encouragement and the reassurance that each of us is truly a Dancing Spirit living in relationship with all others.

New Age Spirituality followers especially use meditation or prayer to reach the core of their spiritual center. They conduct and attend special seminars and create tapes and C.D.'s to facilitate their meditation and use special prayers and words or phrases to help them. Even their music is used to help them reach deep within in order to make contact with the spiritual core of life. Like Quantum Physics research, they find the truth deep within.

Just as are both Eastern and Western religions, New Age Spirituality is open to what Quantum Physics research is telling us, namely that fact finally meets faith. In the ongoing dance of life, by encouraging our true self, our Spirit Self, to become "Dancing Spirits" we will find hope and joy both here and hereafter.

6

Fact and Faith Dance Together
At Last

"Now faith is the assurance of things hoped for,
the conviction of things not seen."

—*The Bible:* Hebrews 11:1

The opening sentence of the eleventh chapter of the book of Hebrews in the Christian New Testament, quoted above, is a classic definition of faith. Webster's Dictionary puts it in similar fashion in one of its definitions: "firm belief in something for which there is no proof." Hebrews then goes on to a more explicit explanation: "By faith we understand…that what is seen was made out of things which do not appear."[1] On that basis, people of every color, culture and corner of the world have believed in God, a Supreme Source or invisible power, and searched for ways to understand and interrelate with that Source. They have accepted on faith that what is visible is made from that which is invisible.

Now Quantum Physics research gives us fact that what is visible is truly made from that which is invisible. It verifies and reinforces that our faith is not in vain. That which is visible is truly made from that which is invisible. Fact and faith dance together at last.

Yes, they dance together. They don't just walk together, talk together, go together. They literally dance together. Webster's Dictionary gives a number of definitions for dance. Two of the better ones are, "a series of rhythmic and patterned movements," and "to move or seem to move up and down or about in a quick and lively manner." To dance together then is to move together in quick and lively fashion with rhythmic and patterned movements.

That describes exactly what happens when those tiny, smaller-than-microscopic subatomic entities are studied. As the specially designed accelerators, which are used to observe them, speed up their movements, those small invisible entities of life set the dancing pattern or paradigm for life that is visible. As they dance, the more they touch others in their dance, the more often they seem to disintegrate, to sacrifice themselves. And as they do, they emit life-enhancing energy, create new entities and resurrect. They never die. They just keep dancing and creating and resurrecting. That is the fact of Quantum Physics. That is the fact of invisible life, the "things which do not appear," to requote the definition of faith in the book of Hebrews.

It is also the paradigm for visible life, the ideal pattern of the dance we perform as we move through each day. Imagine what it would look like if, like you speed up the tape on your VCR to skip the commercials in a favorite program you taped earlier, you sped up a day of your life. What would it look like as you touched other lives throughout your day? Would it be graceful or awkward, grace-giving or careless?

Now, remember that our visible physical bio-body suit is only a "coverall" for our everlasting Spirit, for "that what is seen is made out of things which do not appear," to quote the definition of faith from the Bible's book of Hebrews again. Quantum Physics or Quantum Mechanics, as it is often termed, has established the pattern, the paradigm. The more those invisible tiny subatomic entities which make up our invisible Spirit touch others, the more life enhancing energy is given off. That means that each of us, guided by our "Dancing Spirit," can offer new hope and new life to those around us and, at the same time, actually resurrect into a newer, fresher more vibrant person.

The problem now becomes how can I encourage those tiny subatomic entities, which make up the real me, dance so that I may live with others more gracefully, more grace-giving? Before we continue, let's clarify exactly what it is we mean by living gracefully and grace-giving.

The word grace comes from the Latin "gratia" which means favor or charm. To move gracefully is to move with a certain charm or seemingly effortless movement. Grace-giving refers to the favor aspect of grace. For Christians, grace is thought of as God's love for us even when we don't deserve it. In that sense, grace-giving is to offer something of value to someone whether they deserve it or not, to reach out in love to someone even though they may be unlovable.

How do we do that? How do we dance through life gracefully yet grace-giving? Why would we want to be graceful and grace-giving "Dancing Spirits?" The "why" is explained through Quantum Mechanics, which gives us the factual pattern of how the basic elements of life sacrifice and resurrect while creating and giving off life-enhancing energy as they dance together. To reinforce that, we'll review just how Quantum Mechanics shows us factually what has always been accepted by faith. Then we'll concentrate on the "how," how we can learn to be "Dancing Spirits" who dance gracefully and grace-giving through life, how we can refresh our own everlasting, ever-loving Spirit as well as create new life for others. But first, let's review Quantum Mechanics and the faiths of the world from prehistoric times to our twenty-first century.

We'll look at each basic principle which Quantum Physics research has revealed and reinforced about the subatomic entities which are the essential basis of life. Then we'll match up each basic principle with the beliefs of the world's major religions—Hinduism, Buddhism, Taoism, Judaism, Christianity, Islam and New Age Spirituality. Hopefully, this review will help us find answers to some of the following questions.

Do the facts of Quantum Mechanics research reinforce the faith of millions around the earth, reaching back into the myths and mysteries of the past and, so important, guiding us into the future? Can the facts truly rekindle our faith in the beliefs which may have sustained us throughout our life so far? Can they help us to hear a sweeter music for our "Dancing Spirits" and so look forward with more hope and joy not only in this life but hereafter as well? Whether you are young and doubting or old and hurting…a believer or a doubter…successful or struggling, I believe that knowing fact and faith have merged can awaken and enliven your "Dancing Spirit" and give you new hope and joy here and hereafter. Let's review the facts with the faiths.

1. **The unity of the universe**: No single subatomic entity lives in isolation but only in a dancing relationship with others, even non-locally or faster than the speed of light. This indicates the wholeness and unity of our entire universe, setting the original pattern for humanity to live together on earth and suggesting the reality and unity of the seen and the unseen.

Eastern World Religions: Hinduism has as a basic belief that the entire universe is one reality. They call that reality Brahman and, just as Christians view the Holy Spirit as being available to each individual, so Hindus view Brahman as being in the individual also and call that presence Atman.

Buddhism goes even beyond Hinduism in its belief in unity. Buddhists believe that the goal for which each individual should strive is to blend into Dharmakaya or ultimate reality. Dharmakaya is best described as that ultimate indivisible reality of which all things are a part.

Taoism, like both Hinduism and Buddhism, stresses the unity of the universe. It does so explicitly in its writings, for example, the 25th verse of the *Tao Te Ching*:

Something there is, whose veiled creation was
Before the earth or sky began to be;
So silent, so aloof and so alone,
It changes not, nor fails, but touches all.

Western World Religions: Judaism, while it does not reflect the unity of all reality in the same manner as do the Eastern World religions, offers many passages from Hebrew Scriptures which indicate the unity of creator and created. For example:

> *"And I will put my spirit within you, and cause you to walk in my statutes and be careful to observe my ordinances."*

> —Ezekiel 36:27

Further, Judaism exhibits humanity bound together in common commitment that is unique. Its followers, wherever they may settle in the world, appear to exist in a dancing relationship of mutual need and fulfillment, as though acting out the pattern set by those subatomic entities in Quantum Mechanics research.

Christianity has as its core the teachings and life of Jesus. He lived, died and remains a living symbol of the unity of all humanity. As for the unity of the entire universe, Christians have branched out beyond both Judaism and Islam in their concept of God as the trinity of Father, Son and Spirit. This makes it possible to more easily understand how the creator works in and through the created. It was Jesus who first pointed us in that direction with references to the role of Spirit in our lives when, for example, he said:

> *"...for it is not you who speak, but the Spirit...speaking through you."*

> —Matthew 10:20.

Verses like this give us the assurance that the created may become creators, empowered by God, the Source of all reality, illustrating the unity of all that is, seen and unseen.

Islam also offers some profound passages on the subject of the unity of all that is both in the *Koran* and in the literature of those who study Islam. For example, to quote from a description of the *hajj*, rite of circumambulating the Kabah, shrine of the One God in Mecca, given by the late Iranian philosopher Ali Shariati:

"As you approach the centre, the pressure of the crowd squeezes you so hard that you are given a new life....you are now alive and eternal...The Kabah is the world's sun whose face attracts you into its orbit. You have become part of this universal system...You have been transformed into a particle that is gradually melting and disappearing."[2]

New Age Spirituality: New Agers tend to be very emphatic about their beliefs. The message they put out is loud and clear. Not only do they believe that we are individual members of the same family, no matter what our color, culture or language, but we are all responsible for the entirety of creation. Spotted owl, killer whale or grey wolf, they are our responsibility. Water supply, clean air, naturally grown food, all are our responsibility.

Since New Agers rejected the established religions of the twentieth century, the question arises as to where and how they developed so strong an acceptance of the unity of all reality. That, of course, is where the influence, especially of Buddhism on the west coast of the United States, comes in. In addition, there was the nature of the research in Quantum Physics which impacted the ideas of the relationship between religion and science. As a result of the influence of both Buddhism and Quantum Mechanics, many New Agers view the spiritual as being just as real as the physical. They believe in a definite unity of the universe, seen and the unseen.

2. **Matter converts to energy and energy cannot be destroyed:** Subatomic particles change form in their dancing relationship with each other, sacrificing themselves, then resurrecting as they give off energy as a streak of light and also create new entities. Just so each of us continually changes who we are as our Spirit lives in a dancing relationship with those around us. We, too, sacrifice our egos as we relate to others, give off energy and resurrect a new and happier individual. As matter is transformed into energy in the laboratory and that energy can never be destroyed, so we may be transformed, but we can never be destroyed. Our Spirit, which is pure energy, like a streak of light, lives forever. Our faith promises us that and now fact confirms it.

Eastern World Religions: Hinduism advocated sacrifice as a recurring theme in one of its early important rituals. It stressed that there can be no life without sacrifice. Then there are the stories in Hinduism's famous *Bhagavad Gita*, Song of the Blessed Lord. One in particular on the subject of self-sacrifice is about the god Krishna appearing as a charioteer for a warrior. Krishna tells the warrior:

> "I am the Sacrifice! I am the Prayer!...
> Clasp Me with heart and mind! So shalt thou dwell
> Surely with me on high..."

Here Krishna, as did Jesus, willingly sacrifices himself, promising new life to others. It's almost as though this were a preview of what Quantum Mechanics would show as the basic pattern of life. Matter is converted to energy and that energy can never be destroyed.

Buddhism, also, accepts sacrifice of the needs and desires of the physical body and personality as necessary to achieve the fulfillment which they call Nirvana. This in no way eliminates their belief in reincarnation. For them, the physical matter of life converts continuously to energy and that energy can never be destroyed. In view of these basic beliefs, so in harmony with the past century's research in Quantum Mechanics, it is understandable that some physicists, also familiar with Eastern religions, would see the resemblance.

Taoism has as its basic belief the concept of Tao, the original, ultimate and indefinable reality, similar to the Hindu Brahman, the Buddhist Dharmakaya or our Christian God. It is also seen as the cosmic process in which all creation is involved as a continuous flow and change, like the ongoing dance of the sub-atomic particles in Quantum Mechanics.

The best illustration of what it means to follow the Tao can be found in some of the verses in their *Tao Te Ching*, which is hauntingly like the writings of other religions. For example, verse 7 which we quoted earlier:

> The Wise Man chooses to be last
> And so becomes the first of all;
> Denying self, he too is saved.
> For does he not fulfillment find
> In being an unselfish man?

It sounds like the Taoist version of Jesus' words centuries later, "If anyone would be first, he must be last of all and servant of all:"—Mark 9:35.

Taoists, like Hindus and Buddhists, believe in the sacrifice of one's own needs as well as recognize the continuous conversion of matter to energy, which is never destroyed.

Western World Religions: Judaism, from its earliest days, understood self-lessness and sacrifice. I remember particularly from my childhood reading the story of Abraham and his beloved son Isaac in our second grade Bible History book. According to the story, God wished to test the faithfulness and obedience of Abraham, so he commanded Abraham to sacrifice his son. For Abraham, self-sacrifice would have been easier but he prepared to obey the command of God to sacrifice Isaac.

I can never forget the picture of young Isaac in our Bible History book. He was lying on a stone altar and Abraham, knife in hand, stood above him. All I could think of was, "Not my Daddy! My Daddy wouldn't do that to me no matter what God told him!" Of course, God stopped Abraham and an animal appeared in the bushes for the actual sacrifice.

Yes, Judaism has always understood sacrifice. Through the pogroms and holocausts of history, the followers of Judaism have exhibited self-sacrifice and tenacious love for the life of the entire people. They have lived it and understand the continual conversion of physical life into new life which gives off life-enhancing energy that cannot be destroyed.

Christianity was born of the personal sacrifice of one individual, Jesus of Nazareth. For three years he healed the sick, fed the hungry, raised the dead, championed the outcasts of society. Then he sacrificed himself so that others might live. For me no one captures better than Stanley Carter in *Lord of the Dance* the story of how Jesus lived, died and lives again, as do those dancing subatomic entities which are the basis of both visible and invisible life.

> They cut me down and I leapt up high,
> I am the life that'll never, never die;
> I'll live in you if you'll live in me,
> I am the Lord of the Dance, said he.
>
> Dance, then, wherever you may be,
> I am the Lord of the Dance, said he,
> And I'll lead you all, wherever you may be,
> And I'll lead you all in the Dance, said he.[3]

Those whose Spirit dances through life to the rhythm set by our Lord of the Dance are promised the miracle of new life, a life which cannot be destroyed.

Islam teaches that it is wrong to build up wealth individually but rather good to share wealth by giving to the poor, to sacrifice for others. The ritual known as the *hajj*, which each Muslim is encouraged to make at least once in a lifetime, illustrates the dedication to self-sacrificial loving and living. As the march begins around the Kabah, shrine of the One God, all cry out in unison, "Here I am at your service, O al-Lah." A description of the march not only describes Islam's belief in unity but sounds like what happens in the dance of subatomic entities.

> "As you approach the centre, the pressure of the crowd squeezes you so hard that you are given a new life. You are now a Man, alive and eternal...you will soon forget yourself...You have been transformed into a particle that is gradually melting and disappearing..." [4]

New Age Spirituality: One would hardly imagine that a faith-type movement begun by the younger generation of the 1960s and 1970s would endorse self-sacrifice. Yet they acknowledge responsibility for all of humanity, no matter what color, creed, country or culture and take responsibility for the entire earth as well. Not only the resources of the earth but the endangered species are valued and sacrifice for them is expected and fought for.

This belief in sacrifice for the good of the entire universe comes through in their peace marches, their demonstrations for endangered species or preservation of natural resources, even in their music. I am reminded of a line in the *Simple Gifts* song, "To bow and to bend we will not be ashamed." They actually celebrate giving up ego demands for the good of all in the hope and belief that the entire universe depends on them.

3. **Choices made impact results achieved**: The tester in Quantum Mechanics chooses the equipment used in each test and how it is used. These choices determine whether it is waves or particles which are studied and the resultant actions of those entities. Just so each of us chooses how we use the abilities and characteristics with which we have been blessed and those choices help to form the person we become. The individual is part of the process in science and in life and thus impacts results achieved. The tester is a part of the test and not apart from it.

Eastern World Religions: Hinduism is known for two basic beliefs, karma and reincarnation. Karma is, of course, the law of actions. It means every thought, word and deed, good or evil, results in a similar action which impacts us in this life and the next reincarnation. The choices made impact the result.

Buddhists also believe in reincarnation and accept karma as influencing both this life and the next. They have a somewhat more direct goal however. For Buddhists the goal of life is to achieve total sacrifice of physical life, which they call Nirvana. Failing that final goal, the very attempts at achieving Nirvana can earn for them a better life in their next reincarnation. They are a part of their life plan.

Taoism is based on the word Tao, which means the way or road. It is thought of as constantly moving, like a perpetual dance, and how one follows it determines the harmony and fulfillment one achieves. This gives them the motivation to live according to certain principles, thus being creator and producer as well as star in the drama of life.

Western World Religions: Judaism is especially known for the Ten Commandments which God gave Moses. In those commandments and other guides for living given in the Hebrew Scriptures, Judaism has its guide for living. In attempting to abide by God's laws, Jews become the planners or producers of the drama of life in which each stars. Like the tester in Quantum Mechanics research, each individual becomes a part of the process and choices impact outcome.

Christianity accepts the commandments and uses them as a guide in life, but their major guide to life is Jesus, God's Christ. As he lived, died and is believed as living now in and with all who accept him, so do Christians attempt to live and to love others. While they accept and attempt to follow the Ten Commandments, they are even more mindful of the commandments given by Jesus:

"...you shall love the Lord your God with all your heart, and with all your soul, and with all your mind, and...you shall love your neighbor as yourself. There is no commandment greater than these."

—Mark 12:30-31

In attempting to live by these commandments, Christians become the planners and producers of their lives. The choices made impact the results achieved.

Islam has as its guide for living the *Koran*. Like the *Bible* or the Hebrew *Torah*, both of which it resembles in parts, the *Koran* can be misinterpreted. It can sometimes contradict itself, too, or reflect the times in which it was written, rather than being applicable to contemporary life. Despite that, the *Koran* is a guide to faithful members of Islam to plan and produce a drama of their life, to make choices that have a positive outcome.

New Age Spirituality has adapted some ideas from Buddhism to the contemporary life style with good results. For example, many New Agers accept and are guided by karma. They truly believe that good thoughts, words and deeds are returned to them in kind. And the psychology and "how to be popular" or "how to be successful" courses they take give the blessings of science or at least parascience on those beliefs.

Even more surprising, they even accept the ideas of angels and spirit guides and God, though they may think of and describe God differently from the way their parents have always done. As a result of their belief in karma, they make positive choices they believe can bring about positive results.

4. **The truth is found deep within**: Quantum Mechanics discovered the basic dancing entities of life by research at greater depths than ever thought possible. Just so humans meditate and pray, reaching deep within to find the truth, the encouragement and reassurance to be a Dancing Spirit. As scientific research reveals the streaks of light which signify life, so meditation reveals the source which offers us love, hope and joy here and hereafter.

Eastern and Western Religions: All three of the Eastern religions, Hinduism, Buddhism and Taoism, practice meditation. While the Western religions of Judaism, Christianity and Islam, sometimes known as the religions of the "Book," advocate prayer and the custom of reading their "Book" aloud in group worship, there is a difference.

Eastern religions meditate to make contact with the spiritual, believing that one can never understand life through the intellect. Western religions, on the other hand, through the centuries have concentrated on trying to understand concepts conceived many centuries ago and often not written down until centuries later. They pray for understanding and for help in living according to what has been written, but they continually discuss and debate about what the writings mean.

Only on the fringes of Western religion have we sometimes found the "spirit-seekers," those who try or have tried and sometimes found the voice of God within. A search of the history of Western religion reveals them and today they are amongst those who use "centering prayer," which is simply a Christian name for meditation, to search in the depths of being for the voice of God and for their own "Spirit," which they sense and hope is really there.

New Age Spirituality: In frustration over not having their spiritual needs met with intellectual concepts of God and outmoded religious rituals, New Agers have turned to the East for guidance. The Eastern practice of meditation to reach the spirit within, whether it's the Spirit of God, a Spirit Guide or one's own "Spirit," has taken precedence. And many fringe New Agers, really frustrated old-timers searching for hope and joy, have followed along.

Like the researchers in Quantum Mechanics who delve into the true basic reality of life, so do the New Agers and the old timers who use meditation or centering prayer. In fact, most everyone does that especially in times of deep anxiety and fear. It has been the eternal search of humanity to find the true reality of both the visible and the invisible, the physical and the spiritual dimensions of life, and meditation and centering prayer enables us in our search.

◆   ◆   ◆

Beyond the four major points just reviewed which bring science and religion together, there is one more important area where Quantum Mechanics and spirituality unite. It concerns the dimensions of space and time and their importance in understanding the spiritual dimension of reality.

<u>**Space and time merge into space/time**</u> in both Quantum Mechanics research and in the invisible spiritual plane of life. The reason is that basic entities of life dance so rapidly they cannot be observed in a specific space at a specific time. We only know they exist because of the flashes of light or energy which they give off as they dance together in the dance of life. The result in the physical dimension of life is often seemingly unexplainable happenings, such as simultaneous thought and action occurring at vast distances.

No matter whether one is religious or not, the merging of space/time is difficult to conceive of in our physical life. Nothing physical that we deal with daily moves so fast that it can't be specifically located at any set time.

It may become possible, however, if one views it from the perspective of thought. I was first challenged to think this when I started to write a book on prayer some fifteen years ago and finally gave up in despair. That led me to the conclusion that prayers are thought waves, which I am now convinced is true.

Conversely, all religions still tend to deal with and subscribe to the concept of a timeless infinity. Eastern religions picture infinity through such symbols or concepts as Hinduism's dancing God Shiva, the Buddhists' Wheel of Life or the Tao, which followers believe existed even before our earth.

Western religions, with their tendency to intellectualize, fail to expand greatly on the concept of infinity. For me the picture of heaven, as it was presented in school when I was a child, or even now when glossed over in sermons, seems boring. The idea of harp-playing angels and continual feasting with friends is not my preference. I prefer the challenges of physical life, the successes from which to view the goodness of life and the valleys from which to view the mountains still there to climb.

New Agers, on the other hand, have reached out beyond the established religions to find their own concept of infinity. They have done so through meditation, the experiences of those who are gifted in channeling to the spiritual plane of life, in the work of skilled psychiatrists and psychotherapists who use regressive hypnosis to help patients recall former lives, and finally through the research in Quantum Mechanics. For New Agers, as well as for physicists, the concept of space/time merging is understandable and explains some of the seemingly unexplainable happenings which we'll learn about in the chapter on "Rave Reviews…"

We close this chapter with the quotation with which we opened:

> *"Now faith is the assurance of things hoped for, the conviction of things not seen…what is seen was made out of things which do not appear."*
>
> —Hebrews 11:1, 3.

Fact from the research of Quantum Physics has verified the truth of our faith. What is seen is made from that which is not seen. Our bio-body is only a "coverall" for the "Dancing Spirit" within, which is designed to dance in hope and joy both in this physical life and for the life to which we look forward. It is a life, I believe, which will reward us with opportunities we never could dream possible, and I think there are many stories to tell which indicate that truth. They are stories from, by and about people who were willing to go as deep into the spiritual realm as Quantum Physicists have and continue to go in the physical realm.

7

Rave Reviews as Spirits Dance

Nobel physicist wins prize for spiritual effort
"Science and religion are converging," professor says.
Charles Townes, University of California professor, who
shared the Nobel Prize in physics in 1964 for his work in
quantum electronics and then startled the scientific world
by suggesting that religion and science were converging, was
awarded the $1.5 million Templeton Prize for progress in
spiritual knowledge.

—South Florida Sun-Sentinel
March 10, 2005

News articles, like that from which our opening excerpt was taken, illustrate that science and religion are coming together. Nor is this an isolated incident. In the October 6, 2004 issue of the same newspaper the following news was announced: "Americans share physics prize…Three Americans who helped describe the force that binds together the atomic nucleus were named winners of the Nobel Prize in Physics…they explained why the theoretical constituents of the neutrons and protons that make up the nucleus, could never be seen apart from one another. Their work paved the way for a theory known by the fanciful-sounding name quantum chromodynamics, part of a suite of theories…that explain all the forces of nature except gravity. It also raised hopes that physicists might yet find a single unified theory of nature."

Meanwhile in religion, as well as on the scientific front, well-known authors and lecturers stress the basic truths of all religious and spiritual thinking. Amongst them are Dr. Wayne Dyer, author and frequent lecturer on PBS television. In a recent program he spoke of his latest book, *The Power of Intention*,[1] and pointed out that doing acts of kindness actually creates a feeling of well-being which has proven to strengthen the immune system. He went on to state that wanting more for others than you want for yourself, staying in rapport with God who is your energy source, is like bringing the energy of God to all with whom you come in contact.

Deepak Chopra, lecturer and author of *How to Know God*,[2] believes that the brain is hard-wired to know God and, that as we make sense of the swirling "quantum soup," we inevitably find the face of God. One commentator had this to say about *How to Know God*: "...a brilliant, scholarly yet lyrical synthesis of neuroscience, quantum physics, personal reminiscence, and Eastern, Western, and spiritual thinking."[3]

Karen Armstrong, former nun who became a religious scholar and author of *The History of God*,[4] one of the major reference sources for this book, wrote an article for a widely circulated national magazine.[5] In it she states that "Human beings by nature seek ecstasy, a word that comes from the Greek *ekstasis*, meaning 'to stand outside' the self...Religious leaders claim that the practice of the golden rule can give us an experience of ecstasy...The late Rabbi Abraham Joshua Heschel once remarked that when we put ourselves at the opposite pole of ego, we are in the place where God is."

New Age Spirituality goes even further by joining up with Quantum Mechanics in the recent movie "What the Bleep Do We Know?" Part documentary and part story, it deals with the spiritual aspects of Quantum Mechanics and shows how the world of Quantum Mechanics impacts our normal reality. Through the comments of fourteen top scientists and mystics who participate in the film, science and religion merge as both seem to describe the same phenomena. Some of the truths which the movie stresses and which clearly indicate the relationship between the latest findings in Quantum Mechanics and spirituality, between fact and faith, include:

- Our thoughts and intentions can bring about chemical changes in our bodies.

- We actually can recreate who we are by our thoughts and intentions.

- We are all of the same whole, all Spirit of the Spirit totality, all interconnected.

It is apparent from just these few examples that the merging of science and religion is being reviewed and studied in depth by professionals from both the areas of fact and faith. Physicists, medical doctors, law enforcement professionals, as well as other scientifically motivated individuals, are finding a relationship between the physical world and such spiritual pursuits as prayer, meditation and long-held spiritual beliefs of every major religion and spiritual movement.

On the other hand, spiritual professionals and "spirit seekers," which so many of us are, continually discover now how the research in Quantum Mechanics is actually giving us the factual pattern upon which our faith has been based. It gives us assurance that we may have hope and joy in knowing this physical life is just an interlude, that "the other side" is our true home. We are, in fact, that ever-lasting, ever-loving Spirit, which we've always hoped and had faith that we were, temporarily living in our bio-body suit or "coverall." And, as we have always believed and hoped, the best is yet to come!

But never mind all the accolades. Let's explore what the searchers have found. First, there are the physicists, the scientists, the medical experts. Chief among them for me at the beginning of my search were Fritjof Capra, author of *The Tao of Physics*, and Gary Zukav, author of *The Dancing Wu Li Masters*, whom you've already met and read about in the chapter on Quantum Physics. Then there was also previously mentioned Dr. Brian Weiss, author of *Many Lives, Many Masters* who, after much soul-searching, finally revealed the past life regression story of one of his patients. From the medical profession there is also Dr. Larry Dossey, author of *Healing Words*[6] as well as several other books on the relationship of spirituality and medicine, whom we will learn more about in detail later. We begin now with a physicist whom I learned about while surfing the internet looking for information on science and spirituality. His name is William A. Tiller, Ph.D., Professor Emeritus at Stanford University, Stanford, CA.[7]

My first discovery was an article written by Dr. Tiller commenting on a book whose subject was human intention and thought energy. The title of the book intrigued me but what really caught my attention was the opening paragraph of Dr. Tiller's article in which he stated, "My own psycho-energetic work is dedicated to building a reliable scientific bridge of understanding that seamlessly connects our present-day physics of the physical realm to the more subtle areas of emotion, mind, and spirit." That was exactly what I wanted to try and do but I never could have put my aim so eloquently. He continued with a strong endorsement of the book he was reviewing and followed that by a description of the experimental studies he and his colleagues had conducted.

While my explanation of these experiments will be a radical over-simplification, it will hopefully show the proven relationship between intention, which is of the spirit and mind, and actual physical change. Dr. Tiller describes each of us as a Spirit, wearing a bio-body suit in which our spiritual parents have dressed us. We have then been placed in this playpen which we call the universe. Our purpose is to grow in coherence, develop our gifts of intentionality and become what we originally were intended to be, co-creators with our spiritual parents.

Our bio-body suit, or "coverall" as I call it, consists of several layers. The outer one is made of minute separate particles each with a single electrical charge. The first inner layer is composed of magnetic single pole substances, the second inner layer has to do with emotion substances, and the third inner layer with mind substances. Inside this "coverall" is our spirit-self, the real you and the real me, which is responsible for our bio-body.

What occurs in our lives is that our inner Spirit imprints a specific intention on the mind layer which activates the emotion layer, transferring that intention to the magnetic layer which is then enabled to transfer the intention to our electric or outermost layer. The result is that the intention of our spirit-self becomes an action in physical reality.

With this structure of our spirit-self in its bio-body suit in mind, Dr. Teller and his colleagues designed special experimental studies to support his hypothesis that human intention can have profound effects on both animate and inanimate materials in the physical world. They constructed two physically identical, simple electronic devices housed in plastic cases seven inches by three inches by one inch in size. One of these devices was wrapped in aluminum foil and placed in an electrically grounded container called a Faraday cage. This was the control device. The other device was prepared so that it could be specially enacted upon by an intention of a human person or persons. It was also then wrapped in aluminum foil and placed in a Faraday cage.

Both boxes were shipped on separate days to a laboratory about two thousand miles away where they were each placed in individual Faraday cages until the experiment took place. Four individuals at the original location, highly skilled in mental and emotional self-management, carried out the imprinting of intention on the experiment test box. The group began by entering a deep meditative state in which they mentally cleansed the area around the test box to create a "sacred space." They first verbalized and then mentally held for about ten to fifteen minutes the specific intention which had been decided upon to cause changes in the test box. They then released that intention and mentally sealed the device before returning to their normal state of consciousness.

Three different experiments were carried out like this. In the first the intention was to increase or decrease the pH concentration of hydrogen ions in water. The pH is usually associated with acidity or alkalinity. They were completely successful in this goal.

The second experiment was to increase a chemical ratio in developing fruit fly larva so that they would be more fit and have a reduced development time to reach the adult fly stage. This, too, was successfully achieved.

The final experiment had the intention of energizing the in-vitro thermodynamics activity of the liver enzyme alkaline phosphatase by a significant amount. This was done with an increase of about twenty percent. Dr. Tiller's purpose was achieved. The experiments indicated the possibilities and potential for human transformation through intentions and the energy they create which can impact physical reality.[8]

Dr. Tiller contributed his ground-breaking discoveries to the film "What the Bleep Do We Know?" He also spoke on the subject at a "What the Bleep Do we Know" Seminar held in Santa Monica, California. He pointed out how intention can create thought energy which merges time/space and impacts physical reality thousands of miles away. Further, he said that "…it is time for humans to both understand and seriously connect their individual inner worlds to the collective outer world and vice versa."[9]

His book, *Science and Human Transformation: Subtle Energies, Intentionality and Consciousness*,[10] is considered an outgrowth of his exploration of the intricate interrelationships between the internal and external energy environments of nature and human organisms. What he has proved scientifically is what this book says from a spiritual perspective.

Through our intentions we can produce thought energy which impacts physical reality, even simultaneously at a distance, just as time and space merge and seemingly disappear in Quantum Physics research.

Using the work of Dr. Tiller and physicists like him, other scientists now apply the power of thought energy in psychology and medicine. An organization which brings together professionals in this work is the Association for Comprehensive Energy Psychology (ACEP). One member of this group, Gregory Nicosia, Ph.D.,[11] made a presentation which explained the work of leading physicists in the field of thought energy and how that information can now be used in psychology and medicine.[12]

Dr. Nicosia began by stressing that Quantum Physics has changed the scientific explanation of thought energy and that the physics of today is much stranger than any fiction ever imagined. He went into detail about how physicists have demonstrated that information can travel faster than the speed of light. What happens is that while the tiniest subatomic particles may move at the speed of light, the waves which are present move faster than the speed of light.

This, of course, gave me some reassurance since, early in my pondering over prayer, I concluded thought must travel in waves like light and sound. We just didn't understand how. Now we know this appears to be true, and fact may prove our faith is grounded in truth.

After mentioning the work of many physicists on thought energy, Dr. Nicosia admitted he still was discouraged in his efforts to understand the power of thought. Then he discovered the work of Dr. Tiller. His explanation of how and why Dr. Tiller's work clarified the power of thought energy for him is far too complex for us here but one of his final conclusions is definitely worth stating: "William Tiller also provides us a detailed analysis of mechanisms, the body's bioenergy system that allows for communication between the physical and the subtle nonphysical aspects of our being." In other words, now we know we can, using the thoughts of our physical body and their energy, communicate with the dimension of our Spirit.

Dr. Nicosia goes on to explain in scientific detail that physics tells us how important it is to tune out of our mind the static of everyday anxieties and concerns. Only by doing so can we concentrate on creating the thought energy which can impact change not only in physical circumstances but in ourselves and in other people. He points out there are many ways to do so.

There is hypnosis for regressive life therapy. There are the experiences of mediums or channelers who have the ability to cross over to "the other side," the spiritual plane. Law enforcement departments often have names of persons like this who are available to help as needed. Such methods require specially trained or gifted individuals capable of turning out the static of everyday life and concentrating thought energy in positive ways. For ordinary individuals, there is meditation or centering prayer.

Now, however, we turn to one of the most important uses of thought energy for good and even life-saving purposes. It is in the practice of medicine and the act of healing. There are two approaches to consider. The first is that of special individuals who have the gift of healing or the ability to recognize illness in others. This obviously, according to the Christian Bible, was apparent and acknowledged in the time of Jesus. In fact, many believed then, as Christians do now, that Jesus was blessed with such a gift. Here is the story of one such event:

"Now on his way to Jerusalem, Jesus traveled along the border between Samaria and Galilee. As he was going into a village, ten men who had lep-

rosy met him. They stood at a distance and called out in a loud voice, 'Jesus, Master, have pity on us!' When he saw them, he said, 'Go, show yourselves to the priests.' And as they went, they were cleansed. One of them, when he saw he was healed, came back, praising God in a loud voice. He threw himself at Jesus' feet and thanked him, and he was a Samaritan. Jesus asked, 'Were not all ten cleansed? Where are the other nine? Was no one found to return and give praise to God except this foreigner?' Then he said to him, 'Rise and go; your faith has made you well.'"

—Luke 17:11-19

While there may be many today who claim to be faith healers, a majority are probably not legitimate and take advantage of people desperate to be healed. On the other hand, there are a few individuals who have been proven to be gifted with the power of recognizing specific illnesses in others or of the gift of actual healing. More important to the average individual, however, is the possibility of improvement or even total healing through prayer. Of course, there are many who do not believe in the power of prayer and reject it, along with rejecting even gifted healers. In view of such rejections, any medical doctor who expresses belief in and studies research on the effectiveness of prayer in healing is certainly a welcome exception. We have such an individual in Larry Dossey, M.D. One of the books which he has written on the subject of prayer as a healing force is aptly titled *Healing Words, The Power of Prayer and the Practice of Medicine.*[13]

As an indication of what to expect, Dr. Dossey warns in the book's introduction that his intention is not to prove the effectiveness of prayer in healing scientifically. Rather, the purpose is much more basic, since prayer says something important about who we are and what our destiny may be. He explains that prayer is non-local, meaning it's not confined to specific time and space but may have instantaneous or even retroactive impact. That is also a characteristic of those tiniest subatomic entities and a reminder of the experiments conducted by Dr. Tiller as well. Dr. Dossey goes on to say that since prayer is a mental action, a product of the mind, there must be some aspect of an individual that is non-local too. Something of each of us must be beyond time and space.[14]

While we talk of meditation and centering prayer as being different names for the same activity, it's important as we discuss prayer to point out there are many ways to pray. Most of us tend to think of prayer as an action, something we do. In seminary, for example, we learned what a prayer should consist of. It was assumed, of course, that we would pray to God, usually meaning in Christian context that we pray to God the Father. Prayer, we were taught, should begin with a salutation, followed by an acknowledgment of God's greatness. Giving thanks for God's grace, God's love for us though undeserved, comes next. Then finally we get around to our special request, whether it's something for ourselves, something for someone else or for some special happening. We end by putting it all in God's hands and close in the name of Jesus. It sounds mechanical but really need not be. Most of us find, however, that we tend to pray more often when we're in dire circumstances and formality is forgotten. Even those of us who pray regularly in a vocal, if not always gracefully articulate manner, tend to pray for specifics, even if it is only for guidance or courage, or for special requests for other people whom we care about.

Dr. Dossey makes a distinction between prayer and a state of prayerfulness. The latter he describes as a quiet, inner-directed action which seems almost more like inaction. It reminds me of some of the words on prayer in one of my favorite books, *The Prophet*, by Kahlil Gibran.

> "For what is prayer but the expansion of yourself into the living ether?...When you pray you rise to meet in the air those who are praying at that very hour and whom save in prayer you may not meet...I cannot teach you how to pray in words. God listens not to your words save when He Himself utters them through your lips...God, who art our winged self, it is thy will in us that willeth."[15]

The division I prefer is between vocal or mentally articulated prayer and meditation or centering prayer. In the first we send messages from our physical world to the spiritual world, specifically to God the Father, Jesus, al-Lah, Jehovah or however we think of the Source of all creation. In meditation or centering prayer we clear our consciousness of all thoughts of self or of physical life and open up our spirit-self to the spiritual realm. Instead of talking to God, we listen for God. Hopefully, we will become almost unconsciously aware of some message from the Holy Spirit or from any spiritual entity such as our Spirit Guide or our Guardian Angel.

This is probably the time for "true confessions" from me. Shortly after I began writing this book, a feeling of discouragement and total inadequacy for doing what I felt "called" to do overcame me. I had read and studied so much about all the world's religions, including my own, and read so many books and talked to so many people about spirituality in our world today. As a result I too felt a need to practice meditation or centering prayer. A number of the books I had read and individuals with whom I had spoken suggested that, when meditating, one should listen for and expect a message from one's Spirit Guide. The first thing that popped into the mind would probably be that message. So I decided to try it.

I began my meditation by holding just one thought, "If you're there for me, what's your name?" As I relaxed to soft music, the only thought that stayed with me was, "What's your name? What's your name? What's your name?" Maybe some fifteen minutes or so later, it was as though someone was shouting in my ear, "Dora, Dora, Dora!" It jarred me and surprised me. I didn't nor never had known anyone named Dora. If I had a spiritual guide I at least expected it would have been my beloved Grandma who always called me "Meine Engel in daus Haus," my angel in the house, translated from the German. Or maybe at least it would be my Aunt Betty who washed my hair and cleaned my fingernails on Saturday when my Mother was working. "Dora, Dora" kept ringing in my ears.

Finally, I thought to myself, "Okay, Dora, if you spell it with a double "oo" like Doora and be my door to the spiritual world I'll believe you. "Okay with me," seemed to come back in a kind of disgusted "you don't trust me" tone of voice. I told my husband about it a little later. He laughed and said "Okay, Doora it is. I believe you." We have been married for nearly thirty-five years and he has become accustomed to some of my "idiotsyncracies" as I prefer to call my eccentricities. That wasn't the end of it. In fact, it was only the beginning.

Both of us are continually amazed at how often a helping hand in my endeavors seems to come out of nowhere. A lost book which I need for reference, a block in my writing when nothing comes together right, a nudge at three o'clock in the morning to get up and develop a new idea which popped into my head while I slept. He complains it's cold in bed without me at such an early hour but is grateful, as am I, that something not of this physical world is being so helpful. This chapter is titled "Rave Reviews" and we both acknowledge we seem to be receiving help from some unearthly source so we end up laughing and saying, "Thank you, Doora!"

Whether it is Doora or just happenstance, rave reviews keep popping up from people we meet, newspaper articles we read, or even in stranger ways, reminding us that our long-held faith is being proven as fact. We are given assurance that our faith in the Spirit of God, as well as the blessings available to us from the spiritual home of our own true spirit-self, are ours now in life on this physical earth, and we believe the best is yet to come!

Dr. Dossey discussed several studies which exhibit the non-local nature of thought as it impacted individuals and circumstances and also the performance of certain gifted individuals. One such study had to do with the ability of a journalist who had no formal training in medicine or health but was intuitive in diagnosing illness in others even at a distance. A highly respected neurosurgeon asked her to use her intuitive skills in diagnosing some of his patients at a distance. The results indicated she was 93% accurate.[16]

Another study involved individuals who claimed the ability to heal even though they were spatially separated from the patient. The results were highly significant statistically.[17]

Still another type of study researched is called a telesomatic event. This involves a physical disturbance to one individual which results in a mental or physical reaction to someone emotionally close but located at a spatial distance, a typical non-local occurrence. He reviewed several of these and commented that they appeared to be relatively commonplace.

My husband and I can attest to this. He had been in Haiti helping to install a solar oven at a church-assisted school there. On the road into Port-au-Prince, riding in an open-window truck stopped in traffic, someone had reached inside and grabbed the camera hanging on a cord around his neck. The cord broke but left burns on the left side of his neck.

That same night I dreamed he came home holding a folded white cloth over the left side of his face and neck. When he came home and showed me the cord burns on his neck, right where I had seen him holding the cloth in my dream, I knew! His thoughts of alarm, fear and pain had been felt by me though we were separated by many miles of land and sea. We have had several other similar experiences and are convinced it's more than just many years of living together.

One last study which Dr. Dossey cited and which I found especially significant tested the distinction in results from directed or non-directed prayer. What's the difference? Direct prayer is when one requests a specific outcome. For example, "God, take away my cancer." Nondirect prayer is when one prays, "Thy will be done" or "Help me to respond positively to whatever happens." The most important conclusion was that all prayer was effective. In the comparative tests, however, the non-direct approach yielded results twice as great or even more. That adds up to "Rave Reviews" however you view the study.[18]

To sum up, based on his review of various research studies, Dr. Dossey came to several conclusions.

- He believed that as physicians become more comfortable with non-locality as a concept in science, they would begin to use non-local interventions in medicine.

- As this occurs, he felt prayer as a method in healing would become more acceptable.

- The non-local nature of consciousness would be acknowledged in science because of all the evidence confirming it.

- The recognition of a soul or spirit-like quality of consciousness would be accepted in science as it has always been in religion.

As science and religion merge, humans would tend to pray not just for material or physical results. Instead they would be moved to pray in gratitude for a physical world that is at heart a more wonderful, friendlier, loving place than ever imagined.[19] In my words, as stated in this book's subtitle: Fact and faith would offer hope and joy here and hereafter.

As further evidence of all the positive results of tests in medicine and health in general, more medical schools are now offering courses looking at the role of spiritual practices and religious devotion in achieving and maintaining good health. Both science and religion are stressing the findings that prayer can be good medicine and the positive reviews reinforce that truth.

We can't leave the subject of rave reviews for our "Dancing Spirits," however, without looking at what is happening in New Age Spirituality. You may recall some of what was covered in the chapter on that subject. It is not actually an established religion but a social movement that has to do with the spiritual aspects of life and how they impact our physical life.

Some of our basic conclusions were that New Agers acknowledged the unity of all humanity and our resultant responsibility for each other. They also use meditation or centering prayer to make contact with the spiritual realm. They do so to find comfort, guidance, wisdom and hope to make physical life happier and more meaningful. Finally, we met several of the individuals well-known for their ability to make contact with the spiritual dimension of life and use that gift for the good of others. They are known as "channelers" since they have the gift of being a channel between the physical and the spiritual dimension of life.

One of the best known individuals who has this gift is Sylvia Browne. She has appeared on many television programs including *Larry King Live*, *Good Morning America*, *The Montel Williams Show* and *Unsolved Mysteries*. Of the many books she has written, my favorite is *The Other Side and Back*.[20]

She begins this book with "A Note to My Readers" in which she points out that the book is for you, the reader. It's about the simple things you can do that will make a wonderful difference in your life…about how you can make contact with your Spirit Guide…about your health, your family and loved ones…your peace of mind and your hope for the future, here and hereafter. What she has to tell is strengthened in meaning by her family heritage.

Sylvia Browne was born into a family of mixed background including Catholic, Jewish, Episcopalian and Lutheran, with emphasis on the Catholic. She attended Catholic schools, at one time even hoped to become a nun, but instead settled for being a Catholic school teacher for eighteen years. Whether it was her religious training or the realization she had a very unusual gift, she had this to say about her reputation, "...thank God, so my reputation grew along with my clientele and eventually spread to every continent on the globe. I began to get calls from law enforcement agencies and the medical community, asking for help with everything from unsolved murders and missing persons to physiological and psychological problems that weren't responding to traditional treatment. I was proud and happy to oblige. I've never charged any of them a dime, and I never will. The day I demand a check for helping find a missing child or a murderer, or guide a doctor to a diagnosis or cure for a life-threatening medical or psychiatric problem, is the day I imagine my psychic gift will be taken away, exactly as it should be."[21] Her successes at solving crimes, helping people, reaching beyond the space and time dimensions of physical life into the realm of the spiritual are innumerable.

Another gifted individual is John Edward. He, too, comes from a Catholic background along with Sylvia Browne. It's interesting to note, as an aside here, that the early church has records of individuals elevated to Sainthood who apparently were also especially gifted. Amongst them are St. Catherine of Siena, St. Teresa of Avila and St. John of the Cross. Edward admits to preparing for a public session by praying the rosary and, he says, that he does each sequence of ten beads with a devotion for the people who will be present at the gathering for which he is preparing.

His background is that of a Long Island Italian-Irish family. His father was a New York City policeman. Edward's religion and faith precluded his believing in the spiritual or what some may call the supernatural until he was fifteen years old. It was then that an experience left him convinced that telepathy, precognition, clairvoyance, and even communication with the dead was possible. He worked in a hospital in his early career which he believed made him skeptical about influences on health and illness. All skepticism aside, he has a remarkable record of being a gifted medium or channeler, a gift recognized even by religious clergy who know him and his work.

Browne and Edward are not alone. From the past are the many books and work of Jane Roberts who received messages from the spiritual dimension through a guide whom she called Seth. Ms. Roberts died in 1984 but the Seth books are still popular and readily available. Currently there are also the books of

Abraham-Hicks, the work of Esther Hicks and her husband Jerry. These individuals and their work express the same basic thoughts of science and religion. We are all physical bodies and personalities but our true self is our spirit-self. The quality of our life here, how we live it in relationships with others, and how we think and determine our actions, all shape who we are and who we wish to be. They all reassure us that there is hope for us as we look forward to our return to the spiritual home from which we came.

In addition to mediums or channelers like Browne and Edward, and the less well known who have brought us Seth and Abraham-Hicks, there is the progress made in hypnotism for regressive life therapy. In his book *Many Lives, Many Masters* Dr. Brian Weiss tells of the eventual cure of his patient using this method and of the door which it opened for him and for psychiatry. While he does not necessarily recommend such treatment for everyone, he suggests that it's important for all to recognize there is more to life than meets the eye, more that that which is visible. He believes life goes beyond our five senses.[22]

Following up on the premise that we have more than five senses is an outstanding book by the author of *The Dancing Wu Li Masters*. It is titled *The Seat of the Soul*,[23] and its core idea is that humanity is advancing from being five-sensory to multisensory. It can help us understand and come in contact with our own spirit-self, and will be a guide for us in meditation and centering prayer. To finish this chapter on "Rave Reviews," I'd like to share with you some anecdotal examples of the possible influences of the spiritual dimension on our physical life.

The first is a story which appeared in an issue of the South Florida Sun-Sentinel with a Seattle dateline. A seventeen-year-old girl had been given up for dead or as a runaway. She had last been seen at a teenage party from which she never returned. After eight days, the official search for her was called off. Her parents, however, organized a volunteer search on a Saturday. That night the mother of one of the girl's friends had dreams of a wooded area and heard the message, "Keep going, keep going."

On Sunday morning the woman and her daughter drove along an area where they thought perhaps the girl had crashed her car. The woman said that something drew her to stop at a concrete barrier where, more than one hundred feet down a steep embankment, she barely made out a wrecked car. The girl was found, badly hurt and dehydrated but alive and conscious.

Closer to home, a friend of ours who had been diagnosed more than thirty years ago with Hodgkins Disease suffered a relapse sixteen years later. Fourteen years after that he had a second relapse. The chemotherapy effects left him so ill and discouraged that he was ready to give up. With that in mind, he made a last appointment just before Thanksgiving to tell the doctor of his decision.

The waiting room was empty when he arrived except for one elderly lady. She seemed inclined to visit and struck up a conversation with our friend. She explained that the doctor had told her she had only till Thanksgiving, and he remarked that was not very long. "Oh," she replied, "that was seven years ago." Encouraged by her story, he went in to see the doctor for more chemotherapy.

When he returned to the waiting room the nurse, who had been absent before, had come back, but the elderly lady was no longer there. Our friend asked the nurse about the very friendly elderly lady with whom he had spoken. She looked at him questioningly and said, "You were the doctor's only appointment this afternoon. No one else has been here." Who was the lady? Where did she come from? No one knows but she gave our friend the courage to continue his treatment. He has been in remission for years.

How do events like this occur? For those involved in them, impacted by them, they are factual. Whether the result of prayer or some other power source from the spiritual dimension of life, they happen. And those individuals and their loved ones who are blessed with the results can only add their thanks to the steadily increasing rave reviews.

There is something which speeds up the frequency of vibrations of those tiny subatomic entities which make up our spirit-self. Encouraged to "dance" more gracefully and grace-giving by the thoughts we think and the things we do, they give off the energy of light. And that light is the life of our true self, our spirit-self, which will be everlastingly alive in our spiritual home when we toss aside our worn-out earthly "coverall."

Is there a way? Can we learn how to set our invisible spirit-self dancing more gracefully, more grace-giving? What thoughts do we encourage, what words do we speak, what acts can we do to encourage our "Dancing Spirits?" To perfect such thoughts, words and deeds can ultimately give us a sweeter, stronger hope for here and hereafter but can we really do it? The answer is YES! Yes, we can encourage our spirit-self to dance. Our faith pointed the way centuries ago. Quantum Physics now verifies that our faith appears to be based on fact. Fact and faith come together to give us hope and joy here now, no matter our age or the failings of our earthly "coverall." They verify a future of living and loving in the

Heaven our faith has promised us, the spiritual home from which we came and to which we will return.

8

How You Can Dance More Gracefully

Dancing is the loftiest, the most moving, the most beautiful of the arts, because it is no mere translation or abstraction from life; it is life itself.

—Havelock Ellis
The Dance of Life[1]

The writer of our opening quote was more factually accurate than he could have realized when he wrote those words early in the twentieth century. Dance is indeed life itself. Quantum Physics research now shows us how the subatomic entities of all creation engage in an everlasting invisible dance of self-sacrifice and new creation. Science now confirms as fact what religion has asked us to accept by faith. At the core of our being, we are an invisible but very real Spirit of dancing entities of life. To dance is to live. The dance is life itself and it never ends!

Eastern religions have given out that message since before recorded time. Western religions have repeated the same message, using ideas, words and rites more easily understood and acceptable in Western World cultures. And now the New Age Spirituality movement has delved even deeper into the mystery of the everlasting dance of our everlasting Spirit.

For Christians like me, who are followers of Jesus, we need only think of his words, his life, his death and resurrection into our lives. We can sense at the core of our spiritual being that our faith is now proven fact when we remember words like these:

"You are the light of the world. A city set on a hill cannot be hid. Nor do men light a lamp and put it under a bushel, but on a stand, and it gives light to all...Let your light so shine before men..."

—Matthew 5:14-15.

"I am the light of the world; he who follows me...will have the light of life."

—John 8:12.

"In my Father's house are many rooms...when I go to prepare a place for you, I will come again and will take you...that where I am you may be also."

—John 14:2.

Jesus promised that we would be the light of the world, which is exactly what Quantum Physics now proves. Life is light. As those invisible subatomic entities which make up the real you and the real me dance their dance of life, they give off the energy of light. They not only light up our life but that light impacts everyone around us, giving light to all, just as Jesus promised.

Then Jesus goes beyond that to say that whoever follows him will have the light of life. And that he will be going to prepare a home for us so that where he is we will be also, a promise of everlasting life. This is another Quantum Physics reality of research, since the subatomic entities which make up our true Spirit never die. We just toss off our worn "coverall" given us for our stay on earth, and our true Spirit enters a new life.

As Jesus of Nazareth reached out beyond the borders of his Hebrew culture to the strangers, the outcasts, those who were not of his faith or belief, he set another example for us. All of us, no matter our color, our creed, our country, our culture, have that same invisible and everlasting Spirit. The research of science applies to us all. When he reached out with the comforting words we just quoted, he also told us:

"A new commandment I give to you, that you love one another; even as I have loved you, that you also love one another. By this all men will know that you are my disciples, if you have love for one another."

—John 13:34-35.

"If you love me, you will keep my commandments. And I will pray the Father, and he will give you another Counselor, to be with you forever, even the Spirit of truth, whom the world cannot receive, because it neither sees him nor knows him; you know him, for he dwells with you, and will be in you."

—John 14:15-17.

The facts of science apply to us all. Whether we view the Source of Life from a Christian perspective, our Hebrew heritage, the teachings of Allah, the religions of the Far East or the beliefs and practices of New Age Spirituality, the facts of science are universal. We are to love one another, to encourage our Spirits to dance and to give off the light of life to all, as we live in the sure hope and belief that the best is yet to come.

To help us keep that hope and belief strong, to help us light up our world with love for others, Jesus promised us help. He promised us the Spirit of truth. He even cautions us that in our world, our physical life, we can't see that Spirit. Nevertheless, he promises, that Spirit is with us and in us. We may think of it as the Holy Spirit of our Christian Trinity, as Jehovah of Judaism, the spirit of Buddha, Mohammad or, like the New Agers, as our Spirit Guide or Guardian Angel. However we relate to and communicate with that essence within each of us, it is the everlasting Spirit of God. Let's review.

1. Quantum Physics delves into the invisible world of subatomic entities that exist at the center of all creation.

   We delve into the invisible world of the life force that exists at the center of our physical body and makes us who we are.

2. Quantum Physics has set up experiments which reveal that the invisible entities which make up all creation dance unceasingly, seemingly self-sacrificing themselves as they literally bump into and relate to each other. The faster researchers have made them dance the more they recreate themselves, give off the energy of light and create new life.

   Our life on earth is like a research laboratory where we can set up life experiences in which we live in loving, giving relationships with others. By so doing we discover the faster we encourage the invisible entities which make up our invisible Spirit to dance, the more light we give off and the more light we shed on the lives of those around us.

That brings us to "why" and "how." Why do we want to speed up those invisible entities of our true Spirit that is hidden in our bio-body suit or "coverall?" And, then being convinced that is what we really want, how do we do it? Let's begin with why.

Why do we want to light up our life and the lives of those around us? Why are we here on this physical earth? Why were we born here? Of all the reasons I have learned in religion, from the books I have read, the conversations I have had or in the thoughts and ideas of my own mind, the most profound, wisest and downright happiest reason for me is presented in a book by Gary Zukav. You may recall that he is the author of *The Dancing Wu Li Masters*, one of the two books on Quantum Physics which suggested the relationship between subatomic research and major Eastern World religions. That was Zukav's contribution from a scientific perspective.

From the spiritual perspective he has written *The Seat of the Soul,* a book that builds a bridge between the physical life we know and the spiritual life which the religions of the world have been trying to tell us about since before recorded history. In the "Foreword" of the book he explains how he came to conceive of and write his understanding of the invisible life of the Spirit. He believed it was because of his extensive reading and study of individuals who had made great strides in physics, psychology and other similar fields. He sensed they were seeing something beyond the field of their endeavors and he called them mystics as they in fact are.[2]

Zukav offers *The Seat of the Soul* as a window through which he has come to view life. The basic idea is profound but the book is surprisingly easy to read. For me it is a twenty-first century explanation of what Jesus was trying to tell his followers. It gives new meaning to all the religions and philosophies of life that have been and are dedicated to a hope for ultimate joy, love and peace for all.

What Zukav suggests is that evolution, as we have understood it, has been that of the progressive development of physical life on earth and the requirements for living together. We have progressed as five-sensory individuals, using sight, smell, taste, touch and hearing to live together productively in our physical world. We learned the interplay of cause and effect. A kind touch produces a smile, a harsh word produces anger or tears.[3]

As we move into the twenty-first century we now are moving into the world of the invisible, the spiritual dimension, both in science and in human development or evolution. We must move from being five-sensory to being multi-sensory. Our sensory perceptions must go beyond the visible physical world to the invisible spiritual dimension. As we do that, we will come to understand that our invisible spiritual self has the same interplay of cause and effect on our own Spirit as well as on the Spirits of those around us. Up to now we have experienced the evolution of visible physical humanity and the world we live in. Now we are beginning to experience more intimately the evolution of our Spirit and the invisible spiritual dimension of life.

Zukav also points out that all our great teachers have been or are multi-sensory, highly developed humans.[4] Jesus is a prime example not only for those of us who are Christian but is so recognized even by non-Christians. Through them, just as through Quantum Physics, we learn that life does not end. When we delve into the inner core of life, in the laboratory or into our own spiritual depths, we learn that life is everlasting, a fact which faith has been telling us all along.

Hinduism: Deep within abides another life, not like the life of the senses, escaping sight, unchanging. This endures when all created things have passed away.[5]

Buddhism: When a man subdues well his self…knowing that this body is like froth, knowing that its nature is that of a mirage, the disciple passes untouched by death.[6]

Judaism: The Lord is my Shepherd…and I will dwell in the house of the Lord forever.—Psalms 23.

Christianity: Truly, I say to you, today you will be with me in Paradise.—Luke 23:43.

Accepting the truth that we are multi-sensory, that we can impact our everlasting Spirit, we can see far more clearly why we should encourage our Spirit to dance. It will bring more light and life into our physical life on earth and all those who share that life with us. It will strengthen our hope of a life beyond this physical dimension, a life where joy and love and peace will be ours. It will encourage the evolution of our Spirit to live in perfect love as Jesus taught. What faith has promised us, fact now is showing us the way.

The next question is how. How do we follow through? How do we learn to impact our true spirit-self? How do we learn to encourage our "Dancing Spirit" hidden in the core of our visible earthly "coverall" to dance with greater grace? Actually our faith tells us how. Even those who may follow no religious faith learn it in psychology or human relations study. We call it the Golden Rule. If we follow it, the results will be more valuable than gold. It is found in nearly every religion.

Hinduism: One should not behave towards others in a way which is disagreeable to oneself. This is the essence of morality. All other activities are due to selfish desire. *Mahabharata, Ausasana Parva* 113.8.

Buddhism: Compare oneself to others in such terms as "Just as I am so are they, just as they are so am I." *Sutta Nipata* 705.

Confucianism: Try your best to treat others as you would wish to be treated yourself, and you will find that this is the shortest way to benevolence. *Mencius* VII.A.4.

Jainism: A man should wander about treating all creatures as he himself would be treated. *Sutrakritanga* 1.11.33.

African Traditional Religions: One going to take a pointed stick to pinch a baby bird should first try it on himself to feel how it hurts. *Yoruba Proverb* (Nigeria).

Judaism: You shall love your neighbor as yourself. *The Bible*: Leviticus 19:18.

Christianity: Whatever you wish that men would do to you, do so to them. *The Bible*: Matthew 7:12.

Islam: Not one of you is a believer until he loves for his brother what he loves for himself. *Forty Hadith of an-Nawawi* 13.

The religions have told us what to do but how do we follow through? And what really happens, not in our physical life, but to our invisible everlasting Spirit when we do?

Remember back when we were studying what happens when physicists prepare for research on subatomic entities? In setting up the research, they must first decide whether they intend to study the wave or the particle state of those subatomic entities. Their intentions determine the outcome.

That's exactly what happens with us when we decide to live more happily, more hopefully. Our intentions determine the outcome. Our intentions determine the grace of our dance. Remember, too, the different meanings of grace. In the physical dimension grace can mean an easy, supple, almost liquid-like move-

ment. In terms of faith, grace refers to God's love for us even though often undeserved. When we speak of our Spirit dancing with greater grace, we may actually
mean both, gracefully and grace-giving.

We will be able to sense our Spirit is dancing with ease and beauty when we
experience feelings of joy and pleasure, only to be unbelievably surprised when
we realize why. Yes, just as we have believed God loves us even when we are
unlovable, so can our intentions move us to not only encourage our Spirit to
dance gracefully but grace-giving, reaching out in love for others. Science tells us
this is true!

Our intentions actually impact the evolution of our Spirit. What we intend we
can truly become. We can be a more loving, more giving, happier and more
hopeful person in this physical world now by encouraging our Spirit to dance
gracefully and grace-giving and the result is even greater. Our true Spirit, the real
you and the real me, will have a happier, more joyful transition to the spiritual
home to which the true Spirit of each of us will ultimately go.

As the physicist in the laboratory begins with intentions, so we must begin
with intentions. Just as the physicist's intentions impact the outcome of the test,
so our intentions impact the outcome of our evolution. Having used our five
senses to progress in our physical life, we must now turn to our spiritual sensing
to progress in our spiritual life. Just as there is an interplay of cause and effect in
our physical life, we will find that same interplay of cause and effect in our spiritual life. Science has proven this is true.

Let's assume, for example, that you wish to experience more hope and joy in
your life now. That is your intention. Quantum Physics has shown us the faster
those tiny invisible subatomic entities move in "bumping together" relationships,
the more energy they give off, the more they recreate themselves and create new
life as well. Your intentions, therefore, must lead you to speed up those invisible
subatomic entities of your invisible Spirit. That Spirit is hidden inside your physical earthly "coverall" which, like mine, may be wearing out a bit. Your intentions
must lead those little entities of everlasting life to speed up their tempo in the
dance of life. The faster they dance in "bumping together" relationships, the
more energy they give off, the better your Spirit will feel. As the camera shows
energy as light in Quantum Physics research, your Spirit will feel as though it is
literally glowing.

That brings up two questions. First, how do we know what kind of intentions
will encourage those little invisible entities of our Spirit to glow and dance with
greater grace. Second, how do we know they truly do help those basic entities of
our Spirit to dance. The answer to the first question has been given us not only in

every major faith of our world so far but in secular courses in personal relationships. The Golden Rule says it simplest and best. Treat others the way you would like to be treated. A word of encouragement or forgiveness, a helping hand in any way it's needed, a listening ear, a loving heart, a putting aside of one's own ego for the welfare of another. And how do we know these seeming sacrifices actually set our invisible Spirit to dance with greater grace. There are two ways actually. First, science tells us so and we'll explain that shortly. Second, and even more important, is that you'll know by the way you ultimately feel that those intentions which you turn into thoughts and then into action are doing exactly what science proves. No matter what state your sagging, worn-out, tired bio-body suit is in, no matter how your "coverall" isn't as much in style as once it was, you'll feel better. You'll feel a sense of joy, you'll have new hope not only for here and now but for hereafter. You'll feel the assurance of knowing that pain, anxiety, and your many concerns will end. You will almost literally glow with the light of non-physical reality because you know the best is yet to come.

Before we start "tripping the light fantastic" of our Spirit's graceful dance, however, it's back to science. We should know exactly how getting our Spirits to dance more gracefully and grace-giving works, since it isn't exactly an overnight occurrence. This is probably the time to add, too, that getting our Spirit to dance more gracefully is similar to learning how to get our bio-body suit to dance. Some of us are born with the ability to dance. I have a loving partner like that. Some of us, like me, are born with "two left feet," which my loving partner could probably confirm. Only he wouldn't since he dances spiritually as well as physically. He doesn't just talk about the Golden Rule, he lives it!

Even beyond those who are gifted with special grace are those who have already evolved spiritually to a greater extent than others. They dedicate their earthly lives to the main purpose of helping others. And some are even gifted with the ability to cross over to the spiritual dimension to help others. Even for us ordinary individuals though, meditation and centering prayer can encourage us to free our Spirits so they may dance with greater grace and be more grace-giving.

It is in the research of Quantum Physics, of course, that we have our proof of what happens when invisible subatomic entities are encouraged to speed up their movements in the dance of life. They bump into each other, literally sacrificing themselves, and they give off energy which shows up as light, recreate themselves and create new life, too. By going to the very center of the matter that is physically real to us, Quantum Physics thus proves there is an invisible reality. Just so our body and everything around us that we can see is physical reality. Our Spirit, in the depths of our bio-body suit, is just as real. It is made of entities we cannot see, just as in Quantum Physics the eye or the microscope cannot see the basic entities of all creation. Our Spirit is non-physical invisible reality, just as the subatomic entities in Quantum Physics research are non-physical invisible reality. As in Quantum Physics they dance and glow with light which the camera catches, our Spirit will dance and glow with the light of non-physical reality.

Our intentions are the messages from our Spirit, our invisible reality. They become thoughts in the physical reality of our conscious mind. In Christianity we say it's the Holy Spirit, the spirit of God or Jesus who gives us our good and unselfish intentions. We can't see them. They are like waves of energy from non-physical reality.

For those of us who are Christians and followers of Jesus, we know he told us:

"I am the light of the world; he who follows me will not walk in darkness, but will have the light of life."

—John 8:12.

Jesus is like an invisible candle glowing in the darkness. He lights the candle of our consciousness with the intention that comes to us as a wave of energy. He lights us up. We can then become the light of life in this physical world. Science is telling us how it works. Fact and faith merge.

Our intentions can then become thoughts which we activate through words or in the actions of our body in the midst of physical reality. We speak a kind or a harsh word, we hold out a helping hand or, instead of turning our back on someone, we sacrifice our ego wants for the needs of another.

Those words and actions impact not only others with whom we come in contact physically but our Spirit as well. We see what is happening in physical reality but, just as Quantum Physics shows us that non-physical reality exists simultaneously within physical reality, so our Spirit exists within our earthly "coverall." And just as it's possible to speed up the movement of the subatomic entities in physical matter, so we can speed up the basic entities which make up our Spirit in non-physical reality. We do it through our intentions which become thoughts in our conscious mind. Those thoughts are activated and become words and actions. Some intentions can speed up the movement within our Spirit; others slow down that movement. Here science steps in again and helps us to understand which intentions can lead to a sad, sagging, slowed-down Spirit and which can encourage our Spirit to dance in hope and joy.

Laboratory tests have been done which show the patterns which positive and negative emotions and actions make on the brain, using positron emission topography. To put it simply, positive thoughts like love and compassion are transformed into happy molecules which give one a feeling of well-being. Negative thoughts like anger and jealousy make different patterns on the brain and can even negatively impact our resistance to disease.

Actually, however, each of us can probably tell already without resorting to science which intentions and resultant actions literally light us up or shut us down. Intentions which lead to positive thought and action, such as love, kindness, forgiveness and joy make us feel energized. Those which lead to negative thought and action such as anger, anxiety and jealousy make us feel despondent, shut-down, almost lifeless.

Jesus called us "the light of life" and that's what we are. Light, you recall, comes in different frequencies such as infrared, ultraviolet and more. We are a system of light. Our different emotions and resultant actions represent different frequencies. Those like anger, envy, jealousy and other negative emotions and actions which isolate or turn us away from others are low frequency. They slow us down, they dim our light. Others like love, kindness, forgiveness and other positive emotions and actions where we reach out to others are high frequency. They make our light brighter, speed up the basic entities of our "Dancing Spirit" and light up life.[7]

Every faith through which humanity has searched for meaning, guidance and fulfillment in life stresses the unity of us all and the importance of living together in peace and harmony. Every major faith has stressed the importance of the Golden Rule. Now science through Quantum Physics research explains how it all works and why. All that's left for us is to concentrate on receiving positive intentions from the invisible non-physical or spiritual dimension of life. How do we do it? How do we make contact with the spiritual dimension, with the Holy Spirit, the spirit of Jesus, al-Lah, our Spirit Guide or Guardian Angel?

Some of us more gifted than others make regular contact with the spiritual dimension of life. For all of us, the answer is to pray or talk to God and also to listen. Meditation or centering prayer is to listen. If we listen we will receive the intentions which lead to the positive emotions and actions that encourage our Spirit to dance. The more we dance gracefully and grace-giving, the more hope and joy we feel in this physical world. Better yet, we will more easily and hopefully look forward to our own invisible Spirit crossing over to our everlasting home.

It's not up in the heavens, incidentally. Just as all frequencies of light exist within physical light, so the everlasting Spirits of light live right here with us. Like the invisible sub-atomic entities in physical matter, the Spirits which have left this physical life now live at such high frequency we can't see them. Your loved one, your friend, your spouse, they are all here. You just can't see them. They love you, send you good intentions in your dreams, in your meditation and prayers. Listen to them. They will light up your life here and welcome you hereafter!

9

Dance, Spirit, Dance for Hope and Joy

I am the same to all beings. My love
Is the same always. Nevertheless, those
Who meditate on me with devotion,
They dwell in me, and I shine forth in them.

—Bhagavad Gita, 9:26-34

If I had been asked who wrote our opening passage, I would have had to say that it sounds exactly like the words of Jesus. Judge for yourself. This is what Jesus said:

I am the vine, you are the branches. He who abides in me, and I in him, he
it is that bears much fruit…If you abide in me and my words abide in you,
ask whatever you will, and it shall be done for you.

—John 15:5, 7.

As you can see, our opening passage is actually from the great Hindu Bhagavad Gita, some of which dates back to 400 B.C.E. Words like these, written and shared on the other side of the world probably centuries before Jesus lived, suggest that there have been spiritually gifted individuals in many cultures over recorded time. Some, like the writer of our opening passage, are from ancient Eastern religions. Others are from our Western World religions as well as contemporary New Age Spirituality. We call them mystics or channelers because they are a connection between our physical visible world and the invisible spiritual dimension of life.

For those of us who are Christian, we look to Jesus as the ultimate mystic, since he had a direct spiritual connection with God, whom he called Father. For those born before Jesus or in cultures where news of Jesus did not reach, there have been other individuals especially gifted in sharing the spiritual dimension of life. Each Native American group, each African tribe, every major religion, all have had their gifted mystics. As Jesus has done for Christians, so truly gifted mystics have and continue to help humanity understand the relationship between life on this visible physical earth and the invisible spiritual home from which each of us came and to which our Spirit will return. As Quantum Physics now illustrates, that invisible reality does not change. It is constant and everlasting. We just all view it through what for us is the one and only way. For Christians it is the words of Jesus which guide us:

"I am the way, and the truth and the life."

—John 14:6.

Much as we differ as to from whom we accept the truth of the spiritual dimension of life, and much as we differ in our gifts to perceive and to fashion that truth into our lives, the way to accomplish the connection seems to be the same. Whether in the religions of the East, the West, or the New Age movement, whether in centuries and cultures long since past or right now, the way is the same. Quantum Physics now verifies the truth of the practice. To know the true reality of the invisible, the unseen, it is necessary to delve into the very center of life. There we find the truth, the way and the life. Quantum Physics has done it in the laboratory. Humanity does it in the laboratory of life by centering prayer or meditation.

Throughout recorded history, in every religion and culture, there have been individuals, true mystics, whose stories are an inspiration. They listened to messages from the innermost spiritual dimension of life, shared them through word and action, and thus changed the world.

For Christians, our source of faith and spiritual inspiration is Jesus. One can't help but think of him in the Garden of Gethsemane. Certainly he wasn't doing all the talking. He was listening to his Father God. Or think of him in the midst of his suffering in front of Pilate or on the cross. The Bible just gives us a few of his spoken words. When silent, he must have been listening, listening to his Father God who gave him courage, approbation and love.

In early Christianity there was Augustine who ultimately penetrated to the innermost spiritual dimension and experienced what he perceived as an ascension "towards eternal being."[1]

There have been so many others in Christianity as well. St. Catherine of Sienna lived in the middle fourteenth century, was born in Sienna, Italy and died in Rome. She began seeing visions from her earliest childhood and then became a nun. The record of her accomplishments for Christianity is legendary. Her writings are amongst the classics of the Italian language and of Christianity. There were others like her such as St. Teresa of Avila and St. John of the Cross from Spain. Their accomplishments and their writings, too, illustrate the power that results to change physical life on earth through contact with the everlasting innermost Spirit.

Few of us are gifted as mystics like these legendary individuals who changed history. While many of us pray or talk to God regularly, to listen is more difficult. Whether we call it meditation or centering prayer, we can listen to Jesus, the Holy Spirit, our Spiritual Guide or Guardian Angel, to our favorite Saint, to whomever in the spiritual dimension of invisible non-physical reality is there to help us. Most of us are novices at this but we can learn. The reward is a richer, happier, more hopeful and joyful life now and an easier, less fearful, more welcome transition to the true home from which we came and to which we will one day return.

Before we delve into the "how to" of centering prayer, it's confession time, however. Just as I admitted earlier that I don't do calculus or explain Einstein's relativity theories, I'm not an expert on the art of centering prayer or meditation and neither is my very supportive and encouraging spouse. When we tried settling down in our twin recliners, put on some music to meditate by, and relaxed, two things happened. He went to sleep. I became restless and moved, causing my recliner to squeak, and he woke up. Our conclusion was that the experts are right. When you plan to pray or meditate, go off by yourself. I should have heeded the advice of Jesus on the subject:

> *"But when you pray, go into your room and shut the door and pray to your Father who is in secret; and your Father who sees in secret will reward you."*
>
> —Matthew 6:6.

Nor has such good advice changed over the centuries. I have read many suggestions and many books on how to meditate. There are a very few necessary specifics but much individuality in the details. One of the best books I have read, a gift from my daughter, is titled *Meditation* with the sub-title *"A simple 8-point program for translating spiritual ideals into daily life."*[2] The author recommends, as do many centering prayer or meditation facilitators, that one choose an inspirational passage and memorize it. Then, when you have chosen your quiet place and position to pray, repeat your inspirational passage over and over again. This disciplines the mind and keeps it from straying to anything other than being open to whatever comes through from one's true spirit center. He gave as an example the Prayer of St. Francis.

What is so interesting to me is that I had been trying centering prayer for some time and the inspirational passage I had chosen was the Prayer of St. Francis. This was a logical choice for me as a Christian but the author of *Meditation*, Eknath Easwaran, is a former professor from the University of Nagpur, India, a lifetime Hindu, who created and taught the first credit course in Meditation at an American University. Despite this, he chose the Prayer of St. Francis:

> Lord, make me an instrument of thy peace.
> Where there is hatred, let me sow love;
> Where there is injury, pardon;
> Where there is doubt, faith;
> Where there is despair, hope;
> Where there is darkness, light;
> Where there is sadness, joy.
>
> O divine Master, grant that I may not
> so much seek
> To be consoled as to console,
> To be understood as to understand,
> To be loved, as to love;
> For it is in giving that we receive;
> It is in pardoning that we are pardoned;
> It is in dying that we are born
> to eternal life.

I can personally guarantee that going to a quiet room, sitting comfortably in a chair, closing your eyes and saying the Prayer of St. Francis over and over again for thirty minutes each day will change you and change your life. The intentions that inevitably arise from your spiritual center will be turned into ideas, words and actions. You will be changed. Your Spirit will literally dance to a happier, more positive beat of life. You will be more full of hope and joy.

This is only one way to begin to practice centering prayer, to tap into and listen to the messages which may come from our innermost spiritual center. Other centering prayer or meditation facilitators, coaches or teachers suggest other methods. There are tapes and CDs available, with both words and/or music to help. Let's face it, listening for us in this fast-paced technical world in which we live isn't easy. Many of us don't even listen to each other, much less to the messages from the invisible spiritual dimension of life.

There is, too, the nagging thought of whether meditation or centering prayer is a good practice. It's not the way many of us have been taught to pray. It's not the one-way monologue that we think of as prayer when we admonish others to pray, or when we ourselves are in need of comfort and guidance. I struggled with all such thoughts when considering the best way to make more meaningful contact with spiritual reality. So many thoughts from my religious background and training came flooding into my memory. So many quotes about prayer:

> *"Lord, teach us to pray."*
>
> —Luke 11:1.

> *"Ask, and it will be given you; seek and you will find; knock, and it will be opened to you."*
>
> —Luke 11:9.

> *"And in praying do not heap up empty phrases…your Father knows what you need before you ask him."*
>
> —Matthew 6:7-8.

Speaking is only part of praying. It's no different than a personal relationship. To listen is often more important than to speak. To meditate or turn to your very center in prayer is to listen to the Holy Spirit, the Spirit of Jesus, your Spirit Guide or your own Guardian Angel.

To be silent and listen, to be open to messages of comfort and guidance from the spiritual dimension of reality, is frequently referred to as mysticism. For some mysticism has a negative connotation. It's probably for that reason some Christians tend to refer to meditation as centering prayer. The Westminster Dictionary of Theological Terms gives this definition:[3]

mysticism, Christian: The experience of union with God by the bond of love that is beyond human power to attain and that brings a sense of direct knowledge and fellowship with God centered in Jesus Christ.

Never one to follow the precise rules and regulations set up for living a meaningful life, my definition includes two exceptions. First, in my research and personal experience, to attain a sense of direct knowledge and fellowship with the spiritual reality of life is not beyond human power. Secondly, the results are not always or necessarily centered specifically on Jesus but may seem to originate from the Holy Spirit or even our Spiritual Guide or Guardian Angel.

Both the past history of certain individuals and present instances indicate many have and many do make that direct connection with the spiritual realm. The results also indicate that humans of any faith or no specific religious faith can experience and benefit from knowledge received in centering prayer. Interesting though is the fact that even where that knowledge is not specifically about Jesus, the content is often very like the message which Jesus shared in his words and his life on earth.

Some of my favorite sources for learning about our spiritual center are the books of Dr. Brian Weiss. A psychiatrist who first became aware of the spiritual dimension of life through using hypnotism for regressive life therapy, he comes from a Judaic background, yet this is what he has to say about the benefits of centering prayer or meditation.

> Meditation isn't merely a means to attain enlightenment,
> it's also an extremely worthwhile process in and of itself,
> for it helps us get in touch with our true selves. Getting to
> know ourselves is the best way to learn, for this is how we
> can ultimately transform our fears and limitations into power
> and joy. The main lesson to be learned in life is to love other
> people...unconditionally. This is the knowledge that makes
> us divine, and it's the essence of meditation.[4]

Another author who stresses a message that reminds one of the words and life of Jesus is Gary Zukav. In his book, *Seat of the Soul*, he tells us:

> Eventually you will come to understand that love heals
> everything, and love is all there is.[5]

And still another who stresses the significance of love as the essence of life is Dr. Deepak Chopra, born and raised in India. He has written some twenty-five books and done many audio and videotapes. In his book on *How to Know God*, he had this to say:

> We are all in the force field of love, but in early stages of spiritual growth, its power is weak. We waver and can easily be thrown off in other directions. Conflicted emotions are at play, but more important, our perception of love is blocked. Only after years of cleaning out the inner blockages of repression, doubt, negative emotions, and old conditioning does a person realize that God's force is immensely powerful. When this occurs, nothing can pull the mind away from love. Love as a personal emotion is transmuted into a cosmic energy.[6]

No matter the background of the individual writing on the subject of meditation or centering prayer, the essence of the message of Jesus and Christianity comes through:

"Love one another as I have loved you."

—John 15:12.

"God is love, and he who abides in love abides in God, and God abides in him."

—1 John 4:16b.

"Faith, hope, love abide…the greatest of these is love."

—1 Corinthians 13:13.

Obviously the essence of the messages received from the spiritual realm of life is the same, no matter who the mystic or author may be. It is positive, life-affirming, brimming over with hope and joy here in this life and looking forward to life hereafter.

As suggested previously, however, not everyone agrees on how to engage in meditation or centering prayer. The basics are the same but the difference is in the details. Here are the basics which most advocates agree on and which I too have found necessary:

1. A quiet private place where you can relax and be undisturbed by anything or anyone, especially a ringing telephone or an impromptu visit.

2. A time set aside just for prayer or meditation with no pressures from other tasks needing to be immediately tackled.

3. Comfortable clothing, right temperature, no physical distractions.

4. Mentally and emotionally ready to relax the body and clear the mind and memory of anxieties and all negative emotions.

For many, these requirements will be rejected. Life is too busy, too complicated, too pressured, too demanding, so it's just not possible to follow through on the basics. Actually, those are some of the reasons why centering prayer can be a lifesaver. Once one develops the habit, it becomes almost automatic to establish the basics. The centering prayer itself becomes a necessity because it impacts all of life, making it more hopeful and fulfilling.

Now we get to the details. You will recall that Eknath Easwaran, who taught the first college credit course on meditation, recommends committing to memory and continually reciting an inspirational passage, such as the prayer of St. Francis. He also recommends choosing what is known as a "mantra" but using it for different purposes and at different times. Dr. Chopra recommends using a mantra rather than continually repeating a chosen inspirational passage.[7]

Still others recommend using a CD or tape with music and a soothing speaker who will help you to relax, breath rhythmically and guide you through a meditation session, always leaving time during and after the message for you to meditate or pray in your own way. I have tried them all, as have close friends with whom I have shared confidences on the practice. Frankly, sometimes I do it one way, sometimes another. Sometimes I begin one way and then change to another. It depends on my mood and needs of the moment.

Since both the terms meditation and mantra are associated with Eastern religions, many Westerners, especially Christians, tend to have a negative view of them. As we have already cleared up, meditation is simply a form of prayer, of listening to the Spirit or messengers from "the other side" or the spiritual dimension of life. Followers of Judaism, Christianity and Islam, as well as New Agers, have been and are true meditators. We all have our special passages like the Lord's Prayer, "The Lord is my shepherd" Psalm, or the Prayer of St. Francis. As for having and using a mantra, we all have been doing that too. For example:

- Jews may use the ancient *Barukh attah Adonai* which means: "Blessed art thou, O Lord."

- Catholic Christians may use *Ave Maria.* All Christians may use simply the name of Jesus or Jesus Christ, Jesus loves me, Lord hear my prayer, or simply Amen, Amen.

- Followers of Islam may use *Allahu akbar* which means "God is Great."

My favorite consists of the first three words of John 15:12, which is printed on my personal cards: "Love one another." Repeating it over and over again, in the early stages of relaxing for a time of centering prayer, almost immediately dissipates tensions, anxieties, anger, whatever negative emotions may be causing my lively inner Spirit to be dragging along. Most interesting about the contemporary use of the mantra to put one in the mood or mode for centering prayer is the actual physical impact the repetition of a mantra has on the body.

The word mantra comes from two root words, *man* which means mind and *tri* which means to cross. Using a mantra helps us to cross over the physical mind and relate to our Spirit deep within. Repeating a mantra sounds so simple that many people scoff at it and think it's just a mechanical farce. In a way, it's like walking to a destination. Each step is just like the previous step. Its value is that it gets you one step closer to your goal. Mahatma Gandhi said it like this:

> The mantram becomes one's staff of life and carries one through every ordeal. It is not repeated for the sake of repetition, but for the sake of purification, as an aid to effort. It is no empty repetition. For each repetition has a new meaning, carrying you nearer and nearer to God.[8]

I have researched several explanations of the impact which repeating a mantra has on brain activity. They involve the frequency of vibrations which the words have on the activity of the brain, sounding much like what Quantum Physics research now reveals. Frankly, it is complicated, but the result is that the rhythmic repetition of the mantra causes one's conscious awareness to cross the border from the material to the spiritual dimension of life.[9]

My own personal experience is that the use of my mantra, "Love one another...love one another" is helpful both as a prelude to centering prayer or just to calm me down and thinking more positively anywhere and at any time. At other times I prefer the Prayer of St. Francis for meditation though I sometimes substitute other inspirational passages. In the best of instances, I gradually discontinue the repetition of either mantra or special longer inspirational passage as random thoughts and pictures seem to flash through my mind. Some seem to have no special meaning but others have been followed up by events and seeming coincidences that have made even a believer out of my practical husband. "That's

Doora again," he's apt to laughingly comment, referring to my fanciful Spirit Guide. But we both have begun to wonder: Is Doora really just a fantasy or are these coincidences really all her doing?

All these pages of Quantum Physics jargon, the history of the world's great religions, New Agers engaging in age-old prayer practices, what does it all mean? The more I read and studied, the more questions I had, and the more I learned. How about you? Does it all make you wonder, too? Do you have questions like these?

- Do I really have a Spirit that's made of tiny subatomic things I can't see?

- Do they dance? Do they dance faster when I'm kind and loving to others?

- Can I really receive messages from Jesus, the Holy Spirit, a Guide or Guardian Angel?

- Are all these scientists, doctors and authors proving that my faith is really fact?

- Will listening to God instead of always talking get rid of my fears and anxieties?

- Will my Spirit really dance more gracefully so that I feel more hope, love and peace?

- Will I really be sure that I can look forward to heaven where those I love wait for me?

The answer is yes, yes to them all. For me, in the research for and writing of this book, and for you, in the reading of it, we have both found that fact and faith have come together. When I was a little girl and even when I grew up, I can remember my Daddy telling me "Have faith, Little One." Now I finally know how good his advice really was, so let's do a quick review.

Quantum Physics research has now shown us that hidden at the innermost center of physical life, invisible life exists. It's composed of tiny subatomic entities which even a microscope can't see. They move so quickly in the dance of life that time and space merge. The faster they dance the more they bump into and relate to each other. They literally appear to destroy each other, yet they emerge whole with a burst of energy in the form of light, even creating new tiny entities as well. The dance of life goes on and on.

Meanwhile, science has proven that negative emotions like anger, jealousy, anxiety and stress slow that dance down. Positive emotions like kindness, peace and especially love speed up the dance. The faster those invisible subatomic entities dance the more energy of light they create.

But how do we know that inside this "coverall" we wear, there really is an invisible Spirit, made up of tiny subatomic entities that even a microscope can't see? The histories of religions, even before the art of writing was developed, have suggested it. The mystics of every religion over the ages have been in contact with and testified to the spiritual dimension of life. Contemporary scientists, physicians and proven mystics or channelers have verified our belief. And for those of us who are Christian, who believe in Jesus as the Son of God the Father and in the Holy Spirit, we have proof after proof in our Gospels.

While all this is true, how can each of us, ordinary individuals, feel that assurance, that sure conviction that we have a Spirit which one day will simply slip over the divide between this physical world into the world of the Spirit? You can't see it but you can sense it. Remember that we are no longer just five sensory people. We are multi-sensory. We can open up to that Spirit within us, open up to the presence of God, the Holy Spirit, Jesus, our Spirit Guide or Guardian Angel, however you sense the messenger there for you. I believe that you, like me and so many who meditate or listen to God in centering prayer, will find your intentions to be caring and loving toward others come alive. They will be more easily turned into thoughts, words and actions. The result will be your invisible but very real Spirit will dance more gracefully and you will be more hopeful, happier, more at peace.

No, I don't expect that every one of you reading this book will find the time in your busy life for thirty minutes of daily centering prayer. Even if you don't follow through completely, memorize a favorite inspirational passage, poem or Scripture. At the very least choose a mantra, just a word or short phrase. Then when you feel discouraged, anxious, afraid, sad, use it. If you can sit quietly, relax, close your eyes, that's great. If you can't do that, use the mantra anywhere and anytime. I remember when I was going through some difficult years as a single mother, I had a mantra without even knowing it. It was a line from a poem I remembered from my childhood, "Do something for somebody, quick!" Saying it over and over encouraged me to follow through on the intention behind those words and that always made me feel better.

Remember my telling you about how sometimes events occur that seem to verify the direction my writing is taking? It happened the Sunday after I wrote that previous paragraph. Our very new and very gifted pastor was giving the final message in a series on the "fruits of the Spirit," and the subject was <u>kindness.</u> To make his point clearly and simply, he based it on Jesus' words to love one another and even to love our enemies or, for us ordinary folks, even those we don't like or those different from us. His solution was "random little acts of kindness" and the positive impact they can have on the doer, the receiver, the physical reality of the environment in which they occur and, yes, on the true invisible reality of our own inner Spirit. To which I could only say, "Thank you, Pastor and thank you Holy Spirit or my own Guardian Spirit or Angel.

Following this final chapter there is a lesson for "Dancing Spirits" to help you begin the practice of meditation or centering prayer. Even if you don't follow through daily or faithfully, however, please remember this: Do something for somebody, quick! Or reach out in a random little act of kindness toward family, friend or foe each and every day. Your life will be changed, your Spirit will be changed, your future here and hereafter will improve. You will know that the best is not only here now but more of the best will be yours hereafter.

I leave you with one last thought and a prayer. Think of the word GUID-ANCE. That's what we need from God, the Holy Spirit, our Guide or Guardian Angel. We need GUIDANCE. Look closely at the word like this: G(od), U and I DANCE. Now, let's pray together:

> "God, please teach my Spirit to dance. You lead and I'll follow. As you love me, I will love others, my family, my friends, whoever is in need of my love and kindness. I will do something for somebody, quick. I will do a random little act of kindness often. Lead me, God and I will follow. Teach my Spirit to dance more gracefully, more grace-giving, here now and hereafter with you and all my loved ones. Teach my Spirit to dance, God! Teach my Spirit to dance! Amen."

"Dancing Spirits" Guidelines

This is a detailed guide to help you meditate or practice centering prayer. You may study it and use it to find the way that is best suited to you and your life style. There are also tapes and CDs available to guide you or you can use a background of soft, calming music to help you relax as you repeat your prayer, passage or mantra. I have even made a CD of my own voice, using the suggestions in the lesson, which I use sometimes. If you prefer a simple unstructured method, here are some suggestions:

1. Choose and memorize an inspirational passage and a word or short phrase as the signals you wish to use to invite the presence of God, the Holy Spirit or your Spiritual Guide or Guardian Angel into your consciousness.

2. Sit in a comfortable chair, close your eyes, begin breathing deeply and rhythmically and gradually relax your entire body. Begin with your head and neck muscles, then move down to spine, arms and fingers and finally hips, legs and toes.

3. Now silently begin to repeat your passage or mantra (word or short phrase) to clear and relax your mind as well as your body.

4. If you drift away from repeating your special words and your thoughts stray, perhaps to a particular problem with which you are struggling, then reintroduce your words. Stop repeating them only if you sense positive thoughts and intentions making an impression on your mind and spirit.

5. At the end of the meditation or prayer period, remain quiet with your eyes closed for a few moments. Then open them and you will feel better.

A Detailed "Dancing Spirits" Lesson

I. Set the Stage for Your Dance

a) Choose and memorize your favorite inspirational passage, prayer, Scripture or the verse of a favorite hymn or song. Not too long, unless you know it so well you never forget the next line. If you do forget, it's best to start at the beginning again. Or, if you prefer, use a mantra, a short word or phrase, instead.

b) Choose a quiet, private place with no telephones ringing or people coming in.

c) Pick a comfortable chair, straight or recliner, just so you can relax in it easily.

d) Be sure you're dressed comfortably. No tight shoes, belts, or collars.

e) Have a glass of water or a few mints handy in case you need them.

f) If you're playing music as a background to help you relax, either have a remote to control volume or adjust the volume to play softly before you begin.

II. Get Ready to Relax

a) Settle into your chair comfortably, close your eyes.

b) Now concentrate on your breath. Breathe deeply and slowly, regularly and rhythmically, until you're doing it without thinking about it.

III. Relax Your Entire Body

a) Now begin to relax your body, starting with your head and neck. Rotate Your head slowly till it settles down comfortably and easily on your neck.

b) As your neck muscles relax, shrug your shoulder muscles and feel that easy relaxed feeling spread downward, between your shoulder blades and down to your hips and lower back.

c) When your back muscles are relaxed, let your arms go limp. Open your hands, wriggle your fingers gently and leave your palms open and receptive.

d) By now your deep rhythmic breathing will have your chest and stomach muscles relaxed too, so you're breathing easily and regularly with your entire upper body feeling wonderful.

e) Move down now to your thighs and knees, as you flex those muscles and gently let them relax.

f) Finally, rotate your feet gently at the ankles, wriggle your toes and let all your leg and foot muscles ease up and relax. You're now totally relaxed.

IV. Feel the Energy of the Holy Spirit, in the Form of Light, Streaming Over You

a) You are totally relaxed and breathing deeply and rhythmically. Now imagine that the energy of the Spirit, in the form of light is shining above you. It will stream down over you and ever so gently the darkness of fear, frustration, worries, anger, all those negative emotions that may weigh you down will begin to fade away. Some sense it as a white light, soothing blue or even golden like the sun. Or you may sense it as an aura of energy surrounding and enveloping you.

b) Imagine the warmth, the peace, the energy and light of the Spirit available to you now, assuring you that God is sending you love, hope, peace and joy, for here now and as a promise for hereafter, where the best is yet to come.

V. Begin your Prayer Passage or your Mantra…Then Listen

a) Begin saying your passage or mantra over and over again and listen for the voice of the Spirit whom God has sent to you. As the basic entities of life are invisible in the laboratory of the physicist, and the Spirit is invisible to the human eye, so the voice of the Spirit is unheard by human ear.

b) Know that whatever thoughts slip in, between your words of meditation or mantra, or as you finally settle down to absolute stillness, they are God's messages. The ideas you receive to reach out in love, to know that God is the energy and light of the world and you are a reflection of the Spirit's light on this earth, they are the voice of the Spirit. Listen and accept the message.

c) Then say "Amen" and end your visit, hopeful and full of joy. Your "Dancing Spirit," a little breathless from the wonder of it all, will be dancing gracefully. God has led and your spirit has followed in the everlasting dance of life. And your only question now can be: "How soon will you teach my spirit to dance again, God?"

Epilogue

Dancing Spirits began with a message "From the Author…" explaining why I was writing this book and what I hoped it would do for you, the reader. The idea that Quantum Physics research could actually verify our religious faith drew skepticism from both religious professionals and physicists. It had been my experience, however, that many Christians, especially those near their last days, welcomed the idea. They found comfort and even joy in the idea of leaving their ailing and aching bio-body suit behind and beginning a new adventure with those they had loved and lost.

While the heartfelt "thank you" from so many of the people I tried to comfort in my role as visitation minister for my church were encouraging, the comments and doubts of both religious and science professionals often discouraged me. What inspired and encouraged me to begin *Dancing Spirits* was actually those Dancing Spirits of life that I discovered in my study and research into the mysteries of Quantum Physics.

Remember the story of Noah and the sign of hope God sent him? All I can say to that is "Move over, Noah. God keeps sending me a rainbow too!" Here is the definition of "rainbow" from Webster's dictionary:

> **rainbow**: an arc or circle that exhibits in concentric bands the colors of the spectrum and that is formed opposite the sun by the refraction and reflection of the sun's rays in raindrops, spray, or mist.

This means a rainbow is the energy of light reflecting off raindrops. It's like the energy of life reflecting off our tears. Why is a rainbow so meaningful to me? Well, from the beginning my birth was a bit of a disappointment. My parents already had a beautiful little six-year-old daughter. I was to be "James." Surprise! I was a girl. Pressed for a name, my Mother chose "Betty Anita" which is written on my birth certificate. For some reason she changed her mind later and that name was crossed out. Instead I was named "Iris Ruth," Iris after the flowers which grew wild in our yard and Ruth for that biblical figure of faithfulness.

Actually, Iris is more than a wild-growing flower. She is also the Greek goddess of the rainbow and considered to be a messenger from the gods. When I learned about that in later life I became much more sensitive to the appearance of a rainbow. In these past few years, as I contemplated and became immersed in researching for and writing *Dancing Spirits*, the appearance of a rainbow in my life has become a special blessing. In times of discouragement and disappointment, it has been like Angels sending the entire spectrum of light rays to shine through my tears of discouragement, a sign of hope.

Several years ago when I began to think seriously about the power of prayer and whether and how I could share my thoughts with others, my husband and I took an impromptu trip to Iceland for a long November weekend. It had been a long and difficult summer and we needed a break. On our first day of touring we took a bus trip along the south coast of Iceland. It was a cold and gloomy day but the waterfalls, formed by the melting of glaciers warmed by the heat in the earth beneath them, were spectacular. We stopped for a closer look at one and to take some snapshots. As my husband was about to take my photo, a rainbow suddenly appeared across the waterfall. You can see it in the picture on the back of this book. Almost as suddenly, it disappeared. It was like a sign of encouragement, a display of the energy of light from the Holy Spirit to reflect off my tears of discouragement.

Soon after that experience *Dancing Spirits* began to materialize. My belief in the power of prayer and how invisible, sometimes even unspoken, prayers actually cause changes in our physical world led to my research in Physics and the study of sound and light waves. Dozens of books and hundreds of hours later, the first manuscript was completed, but I felt emotionally and creatively empty. We were discussing "What next?" one day as we were driving up a main roadway toward the ocean and home. The sky was as grey and cloudy as my mood, but as we approached an incline over a major highway, the clouds seemed to move and a rainbow appeared over the hill. It was like a message, a sign of hope, the energy of light shining through the tears of discouragement.

More than a year later, after some four rewrites of the book and perusal by a discriminating and helpful physicist, the book was ready for me to let it go. My doubts set in again. Would the religious and physics professionals laugh? Would it truly help all of you out there who live in the comfort and sureness of your faith in God? What should I do?

This morning, as we talked over the day's schedule at breakfast, my husband looked over my head at the view out of the window just behind me. "Look," he said, "It's a rainbow!" There it was, in the West over the town, not over the ocean to the East, as we sometimes see them. It arced over from the corner of the building next to ours into a cloud formation. It stayed, arced over my head and my now-smiling face, just long enough for my husband to snap a shot of it.

It was another sign, an arc of the energy of light, a reminder for me that God's Spirit has a visible way to remind me of my current assignment in life. In ancient Greece Iris was a mythical messenger from God. I pray now that this very earthly Iris messenger will bring you a message from the Spirit of God. It is a reminder that, with the Spirit's help, we can all shine the light of hope to wipe away the tears of others. The way to do it:

"Love one another as I have loved you!"

—John 15:12

References

The Bible References: All biblical references cited in book, chapter and verse, are from the Revised Standard Version (RSV) of the Bible unless otherwise indicated.

The Koran References: All references are from *The Message of the Qur'an*, translated and explained by Muhammad Asad, Gibraltar, 1980.

Time References: B.C.E. refers to "Before Common (or Christian) Era." All other dates indicated are after the beginning of the Common or Christian Era.

◆   ◆   ◆

Chapter 1. Come Dance With Me!

All biblical references citing book, chapter and verse are from the RSV.

Chapter 2. Quantum Physics Tells Us Why We Dance

Books

1. Barbour, Julian, *The End of Time*, New York: Oxford University Press, 1999.

2. Capra, Fritjof, *The Tao of Physics*, Boston, Massachusetts: Shambhala Publications, Inc. 1999. (Originally published 1975, 1983, 1991)

3. Ford, Kenneth W., *The Quantum World*, Cambridge, Massachusetts: Harvard Press, 2004.

4. Hawking, Steven, *The Universe in a Nutshell*, New York: Bantam Books, 2001.

5. Herbert, Nick, *Quantum Reality*, New York: Anchor Books, Division of Random House, Inc., 1987.

6. Oppenheimer, J. R. *Science and the Common Understanding*, New York: Oxford Press, 1954, pp.8-9.

7. Zukav, Gary, *The Dancing Wu Li Masters*, New York: Harper Collins Publishers, Inc. 1979.

8. Zukav, Gary, *The Seat of the Soul*, New York: Fireside, Simon & Schuster, Inc. 1990.

Articles

1. Blanton, John, *The EPR Paradox and Bell's Inequality Principle*, "Does Bell's Inequality Principle rule out local theories of Quantum Mechanics?" math.ucr.edu/home/balz/physics, Quantum bells_inequality.html, Updated 1993 and 1996.

2. Cramer, John G., *Quantum Nonlocality and the Possibility of Superluminal Effects*, Cleveland, Ohio: Proceedings of NASA Breakthrough Propulsion Physics Workshop, 1997.

3. Harrison, David, "Quote: *Einstein and Quantum Mechanics*", harrison@physics.utoronto.ca.

4. Hemmick, Douglas L., "*Abstract of Nonlocality in Quantum Mechanics*", Dissertation Abstract, 1996.

5. Felder, Gary, "*Spooky Action at a Distance: An Explanation of Bell's Theory*," www.ncsw.edu/felder_public/kenny, 1999.

6. Thought Waves: "*The Future of Biofeedback and Psychophysiciatry*," www.neurofeedback. *co*,za/Bfeedback.html, 2005-2006.

7. Ward, Dan Sewell, *Bell's Theorem*, www.halexandria.org/dward 15.html, 2003.

8. Warren, Dr. Lee E., "*Has Science Found God in Non-Local Reality*," www.plim.org/nonlocal.html.

9. Wilson, Robert Anton, "Reality Ain't What It Used to Be," *Whoa*, November 1, 1999.

Special Mention

- Murphy, Dr. George L., Physicist and an Evangelical Lutheran Church in America Pastor, adjunct faculty member at Trinity Lutheran Seminary in Columbus, Ohio, and a pastoral associate of St. Paul's Episcopal Church in Akron, Ohio, was kind enough to review this chapter. Author of many books and articles on physics and religion, he was gracious but firm in his comments, and I am deeply indebted to him.

Chapter 3. The East Dances First

1. Dharam Vir Singh, *Hinduism, An Introduction*, Patna, India: Three Baidyanath Ayurved Bhawan Ltd. 1991, p.21.

2. Capra, *The Tao of Physics*, p.90 and Zukav, *The Dancing Wu Li Masters*, p.241.

3. Mircea Eliade, *A History of Religious Ideas*, Vol.1: "From the Stone Age to the Eleusinian Mysteries," Chicago: University of Chicago Press, 1978, pp.20-21

4. *Eerdmans' Handbook to the World's Religions*, Grand Rapids, Michigan: Wm. B. Eerdman Publishing Co., 1982. Raymond Hammer, "Roots: The Development of Hindu Religion," p.173.

5. Ibid. p.174.

6. Ibid. p.175.

7. John B. Noss, *Man's Religions*, New York: Macmillan Publishing Co., Inc., 1980, p.178.

8. Ibid. pp.179-184.

9. "pp.184-185.

10. Capra, *The Tao of Physics*, pp.86-87.

11. Noss, *Man's Religions*, pp.187-188.

12. Avatamsaka Sutra, p.104

13. *Eerdmans' Handbook to The World's Religions*, Wulf Metz, "Buddha—Just a Good Hindu?" p.226.

14. Ibid. pp.222-223.

15. Noss, *Man's Religions*, pp.106-108.

16. Ibid. pp.108-112.

17. *Eerdmans' Handbook The World's Religions*, Metz, "The Enlightened One: Buddhism" pp.234-235.

18. Ibid. p.226.

19. Capra, *The Tao of Physics*, pp.130-131.

20. Dhammapada

21. Capra, *The Tao of Physics*, p.94.

22. Noss, *Man's Religions*, pp.137-138.

23. Buddha Dharma Education Assn. and BuddhaNet

24. Dr. C. George Boeree, *The Wheel of Life*, www.ship.edu.

25. Noss, *Man's Religions*, pp.238-239.

26. Ibid. pp.240-241.

27. "pp.236-237.

28. "p. 237.

29. Capra, *The Tao of Physics*, p.104.

30. Noss, *Man's Religions*, pp.260-261.

31. Ibid. pp.245-246.

32. Capra, *The Tao of Physics*, p. 42.

33. R. B. Blakney, *The Way of Life, Lau Tzu*, New York: The New American Library of World Literature, Inc., 1955, p.43.

34. Ibid. p.44.

35. "p.42.

36. "p.43.

Chapter 4. The West Dances Too

1. *The Bible*, Psalms 149:3, 150:4.

2. Eliade, *A Hiistory of Religious Ideas*, p.162.

3. Ibid. p.165.

4. "p.166.

5. "p.l 69.

6. *The Bible*, Genesis 11:27.

7. Eliade, *A History of Religious Ideas*, p.177.

8. Ibid. p.178.

9. "pp.179-180.

10. "p.183.

11. "p.184.

12. "p.186.

13. "p.335.

14. "pp.335-336.

15. H. Jagersma, *A History of Israel in the Old Testament Period*, Philadelphia: Fortress Press, 1983, p.160.

16. Eerdmans' *Handbook to the World's Religions*, Geoffrey Cowling, "Story of a Nation," pp.280-281.

17. Ibid. p.281.

18. "pp.283-284.

19. LORD OF THE DANCE by Sydney Carter. Copyright 1963 Stainer & Bell Ltd. (admin. Hope Publishing Company, Carol Stream, Illinois 60188) All rights reserved. Used by permission.

20. Karen Armstrong, *A History of God*, New York: Ballantine Books (by arrangement with Alfred A. Knopf, Inc.) 1993, pp.87-88.

21. Ibid. p. 86.

22. "p.100.

23. "p. 87.

24. "p. 89.

25. "p. 92.

26. "p. 97.

27. "p.106.

28. "pp.107-108.

29. "p.111.

30. "pp.113-115.

31. *Oxford Dictionary of the Christian Church*, Oxford University Press, Second Edition. Reprinted 1984, 1985. pp.339, 968-969.

32. Ibid. p.75.

33. Armstrong, *A History of God*, p.119.

34. Ibid. pp.123-124.

35. "pp.119, 121.

36. *The Bible*, John 14:16-17.

37. R. Gagne, T. Kane & R. Ver Eecke, *Dance in Christian Worship*, Washington: Pasdtoral, 1984, p.43.

38. Ibid. pp.36,38.

39. "p.47.

40. D. Adams & D. Apostolos-Cappadona, eds. *Dance as Religious Studies*, New York: Crossroad, 1990, p.21.

41. *Oxford Dictionary of the Christian Church*, p.241.

42. R. Gagne, T. Kane & R. Ver Eecke, *Dance in Christian Worship*, p.59

43. Carter, LORD OF THE DANCE, verses 2-4.

44. Ibid. verse 5 and chorus.

45. Armstrong, *A History of God*, p.152.

46. Ibid. p.132.

47. "pp.132-133.

48. "p.153.

49. "p.134.

50. "p.136.

51. "p.134.

52. *Eerdmans' Handbook to the World's Religions*, Lothar Schmalfuss, "Muhammad," p.311.

53. Ibid. p.307.

54. Armstrong, *A History of God*, p.139.

55. Ibid.pp.137, 140.

56. "p.140-141.

57. *The Koran*, 80:24-32.

58. Armstrong, *A History of God*, p.143.

59. *Eerdmans' Handbook to the World's Religions*, Schmalfuss, p.311.

60. Armstrong, *A History of God*, p.154.

61. Ibid. p.155.

62. "pp.156-157.

63. "pp. 158-159.

64. "pp.170-171.

65. *Confessions IX*, 24, trans. Henry Chadwick (Oxford, 1991), p.171.

66. Ali Shariati, *Hajj*, trans. Laleh Bakhtiar (Teheran, 1988), pp.54-56.

67. Armstrong, *A History of God*, p.225.

68. Ibid. pp.240-241 and various Internet sources of information and promotion on the Whirling Dervishes.

69. *Masnawi*, I, i, quoted in Hodgson, *The Venture of Islam*, II, p.250.

Chapter 5. East Joins West in a "New Age" Dance

1. *Simple Gifts*, an old Shaker song which has become popular for New Agers, in particular, as a much-loved folk song.

2. *The Bible*, John 15:12

3. Armstrong, *A History of God*, p.217. *Confessions* IX:24, Trans. Henry Chadwick (Oxford, 1991), p.171.

4. Armstrong, *A History of God*, pp.218-219. *Confessions* IX:25, pp.171-172.

5. Armstrong, *A History of God*, p.219.

6. Brian Weiss, M.D. *Many Lives, Many Masters*, Preface.

7. Josephus, *Jewish War* (3, 8, 5); *Antiquities of the News* (18, 1, 3).

8. Sylvia Browne, *Life on the Other Side*, New York: Penguin Putnam Inc. 2001.

9. Brian Weiss, M.D. *Messages from the Masters*, New York: Warner Books, 2001.

10. Ibid. p.5.

11. "p.6.

12. *Simple Gifts*.

Chapter 6. Fact and Faith Dance Together At Last

1. *The Bible*, Hebrews 11:3.

2. Ali Shariati, *Hajj*, pp.54-56.

3. Carter, *Lord of the Dance*, verse 5 and chorus.

4. Ali Shariati, Hajj, pp.54-56.
Note: All quotations from various scriptures indicated have source noted and have been referenced in earlier chapters. Christian scripture quotes are from *The Bible*.

Chapter 7. Rave Reviews as Spirits Dance

1. Dr. Wayne W. Dyer, *The Power of Intention*, Hay House, 2004.

2. Dr. Deepak Chopra, *How to Know God*, New York: Harmony Books, 2000.

3. Ibid. Back Jacket.

4. Armstrong, *A History of God*.

5. AARP *The Magazine*, March/April 2005, pp.54-58.

6. Larry Dossey, M.D. *Healing Words*, San Francisco: Harper, 1993.

7. William A. Tiller, Ph.D., Professor Emeritus of Materials Science & Engineering, Stanford University, Stanford, California and Chairman, The William A. Tiller Foundation for New Science, Payson, Arizona.

8. Tiller, Review of the book, *Exploring the Effects of Human Intention and Thought Energy* by Drs. Lambrou and Pratt.

9. Tiller, "Some Science Adventures with Real Magic," Presentation Abstract for "What the Bleep Do We Know" Seminar, Santa Monica, California, February 2005.

10. William A. Tiller, Ph.D., *Science and Human Transformation: Subtle Energies, Intentionality and Consciousness*, Walnut Creek, California: Pavior Publishing, 1997.

11. Gregory Nicosia, Ph.D., B.C.F.E., Member of **acep** (Association for Comprehensive Energy Psychology) and founder of Advanced Diagnostics, P.C., Pittsburgh, Pennsylvania.

12. Nicosia, Presentation to **acep** on "Basic Realities of Thought Energy Therapies, Theory, Science & Applications."

13. Dossey, *Healing Words*.

14. Ibid. p.6.

15. Gibran, *The Prophet*, "On Prayer."

16. Dossey, *Healing Words*, p.45.

17. Ibid. p.48.

18. "p.97.

19. "pp.205-206.

20. Sylvia Browne with Lindsay Harrison, *The Other Side and Back*, New York: New American Library, Division of Penguin Putnam, Inc., 1999.

21. Ibid, pp.XXIV-XXV.

22. Weiss, *Many Lives, Many Masters*, p.218.

23. Gary Zukav, *The Seat of the Soul*, New York: Fireside, Simon & Schuster Inc., 1990.

Chapter 8. How You Can Dance More Gracefully

1. Havelock Ellis, *The Dance of Life*, Chapter 2.

2. Zukav, *The Seat of the Soul*, Forward pp.11-12.

3. Ibid. pp.20-21.

4. " p.27.

5. Weiss, *Messages from the Masters*, p.24.

6. Ibid. p.247. Zukav, *Seat of the Soul*, pp.94-95.

Chapter 9. Dance, Spirit, Dance for Hope and Joy

1. Armstrong, *A History of God*, p.217.

2. Eknath Easwaran, *Meditation*, Tomales, California: Nilgiri Press, 1991, 2003.

3. Donald K. McKim, *Westminster Dictionary of Theological Terms*, Louisville, Kentucky: Westminster John Knox Press, 1996.

4. Brian L. Weiss, M.D., *Meditations*, Carlsbad, California: Hay House, Inc., 2002, p.36.

5. Zukav, *Seat of the Soul*, p.121.

6. Deepak Chopra, M.D., *How to Know God*, New York: Harmony Books, 2000, p.146.

7. Ibid. p.95.

8. Easwaran, *Meditation*, p.62.

9. Chopra, *How to Know God*, pp.93-94.

978-0-595-40516-9
0-595-40516-9

Printed in the United States
110681LV00003B/279/A